STAY THE
DISTANCE

MARA DABRISHUS

Dabrishus, Mara, 1981 -
Stay the Distance / Mara Dabrishus

Editor: Erin Smith

ISBN: 0996187219
ISBN-13: 978-0996187213

www.maradabrishus.com

STAY THE DISTANCE

MARA DABRISHUS

Also by Mara Dabrishus

Finding Daylight

Stay the Distance Trilogy & Short Stories:
Whirlaway: a Short Story
Saratoga Summers: a Short Story

For Michael, Nancy, and Anna.

Chapter One

Horses dot the ribbon of dirt, their bodies shaded by early morning mist. Their breaths plume like dragon smoke, slipping around thundering hooves and disappearing into the watery air. Kali shakes her head, bending her neck until I feel the strain in my arms. She snorts her own plumes and strolls evenly out underneath me, galloping down the middle of the training track at Belmont Park.

I've been given my orders: breeze two furlongs—a quarter of a mile—starting at the quarter-mile pole, which resides on the sweeping far turn of the main track, only strides from the homestretch, and push hard at the finish. Belmont is a giant of a track, and the pole in question lurks in the mist just out of sight. Regardless, I'm primed for it, and so is Kali. She tugs her head further down in great effort to haul me out of the saddle and over her neck when I nudge her closer to the rail.

We've both done this many, many times before.

When the striped pole slips by I slide low in the saddle and give Kali room to go. One moment she's bottled up, and the next she's a stream of copper, her chestnut mane smacking me hard in the face while her strides lengthen and everything becomes a droning rumble of hooves and wind.

Curling into the stretch, Kali drifts away from the rail and then skips right back to it, skimming so close my jeans rub against the solid plastic barrier. I call for a lead change as soon as we're in the straightaway, and Kali explodes forward so fast

I'm not ready for it. A surge of adrenaline shudders through me, informing me that I'd better move with the horse or be content with falling off. I shift my weight where it should be so I'm not left behind, slip back into equilibrium with Kali's plunging strides, and ask for more with my hands fisted in her mane.

We blow past the finish line, and I ease off her neck. Kali huffs and flicks her ears up. I gallop her out another furlong and slow her down to a canter. Kali rocks into the three-beat gait, and I twitch my fingers on the rubbery reins, hangovers from my years of dressage, keeping the conversation going with her mouth through the bit. Kali likes it, lowering her head and moving like a dream.

If we weren't on the track, I'd sit deep in the saddle and rock with the horse. Balance would have new meaning instead of my current position perched on Kali's shoulders with my butt in the air. My crop sticks out of my back pocket like an antenna.

When I ask Kali to drop down to a trot, I finally sink back into the lightweight exercise saddle just long enough to feel the touch of leather before rising up and down with her rhythm. Our destination is just past the homestretch, where gaps in the outer rail lead directly into the track's backside, home of thousands of horses housed in long shedrows. On my approach, I spot Dad's blond head bowed over his tablet computer, tapping away at it in single-minded focus.

"Were you counting through those furlongs?" Dad says when I slow Kali to a jaunting walk. He doesn't look up. The filly is excited, bouncing on her toes with each stride.

"A tick over twelve for each," I tell him, keeping Kali moving through the gap and well away from the activity of horses coming and going. Dad puts the tablet to sleep and walks with me, shoving one hand in the pocket of dusty blue jeans as he studies the way the filly moves.

"The quarter was 24 and change," Dad confirms for me. I catch a small smile playing at the corners of his mouth. He taught me how to estimate my speed on the track, and every so often he still likes to ask. I think it's more like a test to keep me on my toes.

Twelve seconds to a furlong is optimal because it's average. Too much either way is telling, but there are reasons to go faster at any point in a work. The faster you go at the end, the easier the racer you have on your hands. Kali does it all, like the push of a button. Today she did just what I asked of her.

It's a ruse.

"Did the gallop out in seventeen," Dad says.

"It's pretty typical for her."

It's textbook, actually. Perfect. Kali has a habit of doing these beautiful works that never translate during the races in the afternoon. They call animals like her morning glories, or horrendous bets. Take your pick. Right now, I think Dad is searching for a bad morning from Kali in hopes that she's saving something magnificent for a race. So far, that hasn't exactly happened.

Today we'll drop Kali into a maiden claimer, a race in which every horse has never won and is also up for sale. In this business, it's called racing for a tag. The horse runs the race for one owner, but might go home with someone else. Maiden claimers are the biggest class drop for a race horse, going from everyone rooting for you to everyone hoping you'll just go away.

I think about Kali's race this afternoon and a piece of me twists. I can't imagine a morning without Kali. I tangle my fingers through her mane while she mouths the bit, bobbing her head. Right now, wishing for a magic fix to all of Kali's problems is a waste of time. She'll race and she might leave, and I'll have to get over it like I always have. I'll suck it up and act like an adult, just like everyone else.

Nothing is permanent, I tell myself over and over. *Especially not a horse.*

Dad grunts at his clipboard and rubs a hand over his hair, tousling it past the point of taming. I can feel the frustration in him, something that I don't see often. Training Thoroughbreds comes naturally to him, like breathing. Horses seem to give up their secrets to him, willing and pliant the second he puts a hand on them. Kali isn't falling into line like the rest, and she fails in the clutch.

So she has to go.

"Take her up to 27, July."

He slaps the filly's flank halfheartedly and turns back to the track. I rub a hand over Kali's fire red mane and let her drop her head, ambling with a shuffle step all the way to the barn.

The backside is a flurry of activity. Horses steam from early morning baths. Grooms scrub out buckets. Manure and soiled bedding piles high in wheelbarrows as stalls are fastidiously cleaned in rapid succession. It's not beautiful, but it is industrious. I grew up here, learning how to walk and eventually ride, in the backside shedrows.

Dad has been training horses for Blackbridge Farm out of Barn 27 since I was twelve. Blackbridge Farm is a raging hit on the New York circuit—Belmont, Saratoga, and Aqueduct—and well enough nationally to show off a few shiny trophies in the main house at their breeding and training facility outside of Saratoga Springs. Growing up, vacations coincided with the Breeders' Cup and the Triple Crown. Other people's beaches and European excursions were my Santa Anita and Gulfstream Park.

Barn 27 is our Belmont headquarters, and it's currently in a state of disarray. Hay and shavings tumble out of nearly every stall, blue buckets collect along the walls, and the hardwood paneling between stalls cries out to be refinished. The dirt pathway in front of the stalls needs a good raking, and I swear the tack room swallowed the last person who attempted its organization.

It's barely organized chaos, but it's home.

"July!" Izzie yells at me from Barn 27 as soon as I come within sight.

Izzie stands in front of the mayhem behind her, her hands resting on her narrow hips which peek out from underneath her too short top.

"Hi, Izzie," I say, easing Kali to a halt outside of 27, kicking my feet out of the stirrups when Izzie takes Kali's head. I jump off the petite filly, pulling my crash helmet off and untying the bandana that covers my sweaty hair.

"How did she go?" Izzie asks brightly, like she doesn't already know. Izzie takes care of several of the horses I ride, so I see her nearly every day for hours on end. Her two-toned blond and black hair is swept up in a sloppy ponytail, blond streaks falling over her forehead and twisting in a tangle past her chin. Despite the fact that she looks like she just arrived from the Jersey Shore, with her chipped pink nails and smeared dark eye shadow, Izzie knows horses.

"Same," I say, undoing the girth and pulling my saddle off the filly's steaming back. Izzie is already swapping out the bridle for the filly's leather halter.

Izzie tisks, although I don't know if it's directed toward me or the horse. Kali is as perky as usual, swishing her chestnut tail and prancing those long white legs across the gravel toward the hose.

"One of these days," Izzie says, talking to the horse now, "you'll get your act together."

The filly ducks her head and tucks it under Izzie's arm, as if to say, *No, I really won't.*

∾

It's late in the day for Kali's claimer. The chestnut filly side-steps, doing a two-beat jig. She arches her neck against my arm, mouths the bit around her tied tongue, and flicks her ears back while Dad tightens her girth.

"Whoa," I murmur, laying my hand flat against the whorl on the center of her forehead. "Whoa, Kali."

The filly stops fidgeting and lifts her head, making my hand fall away. She eyes the Belmont Park paddock, where the rest of her competition idly walks before the weekday crowd. The hardcore handicappers are in attendance. It's a group mostly comprised of middle-aged men with greasy hair and bent cigarettes held between nicotine-stained fingers. Most aren't really watching the horses; they're studying crinkled sections of the *Daily Racing Form* or battered racing programs. If they're watching the horses, they are staring intently.

"Stretch her legs out, July," Dad says, still fiddling with the saddle. I obediently run my hands down Kali's front legs, lifting each in turn. The filly grunts and lowers her head, nuzzling my tangled bun of straw-blond hair.

"Don't get any ideas," I warn her, straightening.

Izzie laughs. "Dye it," she advises with a wry smile. "Then you won't have that problem."

"Hardly," I tell her. "I don't think I can pull off your look."

"Few can," Izzie shoots back, stroking the crest of the filly's neck and cupping her hand around the filly's ear. She leans in and whispers something softly to the filly, so I cannot pick out all the words although I know exactly what they are.

Dios te salve, Maria. Llena eres de gracia: El Señor es contigo.

It's Kali's Hail Mary. My mother used to bend over the necks of every horse she rode, whispering the same prayer into their flighty heads. It must have made her feel more secure in the outcome, more in control. Izzie likes to keep up the tradition, but I say nothing. After all, I can't do anything once the filly sets foot on the track except hope.

The race has assembled a motley crew of runners from the bottom of the barrel. Right now, someone could have plunked down a hefty deposit with the racing secretary and filled out a slip of paper with Kali's name on it, claiming her out from under us the second the starting gate opens.

My stomach flutters. I swallow, but the feeling stays uncomfortably lodged right in my gut. I wonder if anyone out in the crowd has eyes only for Kali.

"Good afternoon, ladies," Pilar Navarro calls to us as she breaks away from the line of jockeys walking into the paddock. Blackbridge's solid black silks shimmer on her, camouflaging dark curls that twist over her shoulder in a French braid. She carries a white helmet under one arm, and a riding crop dangles from her fingers like a baton. Altogether she is extra tiny, easily the size of Mom or smaller, and everything about her Hispanic features is elfin.

"And gentleman," she amends when Dad gives her a look over the filly's back. "Hi, Rob."

"Pilar," he says by way of acknowledgment. "Have any words of wisdom for us today?"

"I thought that was your job." Pilar's eyes widen comically as she pats the filly. "Kali hasn't given up her secrets?"

"Maybe you'll have better luck," Dad says, since this is our first time using Pilar on Kali. Pilar is an apprentice jockey – called a bug for the asterisk next to her name on the racing program – with twenty wins under her belt and a seven pound weight advantage over everyone else in the field. Seven pounds can win or lose a race, but weight isn't Kali's problem. Pilar likes Kali, and Dad likes Pilar's riding, so here we are. It's time to start hoping.

At riders up, Dad boosts Pilar into the saddle and away they go. The horses file around the giant oak tree that dominates the paddock, grooms leading each toward the tunnel that cuts through the ivy covered brick wall of the racecourse and ends on the dirt track on the other side.

"Ready?" Dad asks me.

I pull my hair off my neck when a bead of sweat drips down my back and soaks into the waistband of my jeans. I shoot a hopeful smile at him, which he doesn't return. "Now or never."

In the grandstand, the Blackbridge viewing box sits empty. Unsurprising for a weekday. During the large races, the owners will pack it full. I've spent countless races crammed into that box to watch our horses run in high stakes handicaps, all of us screaming until our faces turned purple from exertion.

Today we bypass the box entirely, since we don't even begin to meet the fancy dress code. Instead we settle in the clubhouse, where I can prop up my dirty boots on the empty seat in front of me and watch the post parade. The horses trot by in single file. Belmont Park stretches out around them in a massive mile and a half loop. The stands hunch along the homestretch, casting a looming shadow over the finish line.

When the horses have warmed up and arrive at the starting gate the announcer's voice crackles across the grandstand, Kali's full name bouncing off the mostly empty seats.

"Kaliningrad is the last to load . . ."

Even though the starting gate is clear on the opposite side of the track, parked in the middle of the backstretch, I know Kali is eyeing the gate suspiciously.

"They're all in line."

No matter what, my chest always tightens up before a race. A rush of adrenaline spikes all the way down my spine, and it's like I'm right *there*. Right on top of Kali, squeezed in that metal stall, looking out at the dirt with my heart in my throat. The starter opens the gates, and the bell rings.

The horses speed down the backstretch, enter the long far turn, and Kali maintains position in third. It's the best she's done yet, and the closest she's come to the front in all five of her races. A bay mare leads the pack, with a giant gray on her tail. Kali is a length behind them, the dirt splattering up on

9

her pristine white legs and her narrow body aiming for a hole between the horses in front of her and the rail.

"Kaliningrad is making a bid down the inside..."

She goes for it. One minute she's moving easy and the next she's plunging forward, finally running for the lead like we've always wanted. Pilar gives the filly rein and begins to work at her, urging her franticly while the rest of the field begins to drive for the finish.

Then I see it. Her stride doesn't shorten, but it lacks urgency. While the other seven horses are buckling down if they can, Kali practically spits out the bit. The bay keeps her head in front, but the gray is done. Kali inadvertently moves into second while a late charger rallies, nipping Kali, who probably doesn't give a damn, by a solid length at the wire.

Kali gallops out, all gorgeous and collected, like she's not aware she's a racehorse. There's no one waiting for the horses to come back from the race, which means that none of the horses have been claimed. Kali gets to stay with us a little longer, something to celebrate in the short term. Long term is a different question.

She's still a maiden filly, lacking a win and any effort to try. We'll reset the clock and begin the process all over again tomorrow.

I let out a breath. At least there will be a tomorrow.

"We'll figure her out," Dad says, giving my shoulder a squeeze as we walk out onto the trackside apron to watch the horses arrive back at the grandstand. Izzie collects Kali while the winning filly is led into the winner's circle, a small crowd of supporters clustering in front of the track photographer.

I turn around, uninterested in the winning filly or the way Kali looks after the race. A gaggle of co-eds leaves one of the food stands nearby with plastic cups of beer, the contents sliding down their fingers and pattering the apron floor. My stomach grumbles, and I remember how little I've eaten since shoving half a donut down my throat between rides.

"Food," I say simply to Dad, who nods and says, "I'll be in 27."

The food stand has hot dogs, and I liberally coat mine in mustard before inhaling it greedily and licking my fingers on my way past the weather worn picnic tables. Men sit out in the sun at each table, taking up space with their racing programs and ashtrays. The backs of their necks are red from the sun, and the more careless have their shirts half buttoned to vent the early summer heat. One looks up from under his fedora and locks eyes on me.

"You're Carter's kid?" he asks, as if he doesn't already know. This guy is a lifer, the kind of man who gets up early to buy the *Form*, make his picks, and collects his winnings in a shoebox he probably keeps under his bed. We all know the lifers.

He points with his cigarette at the track. "That one needs a stronger rider. No bug boy is going to get it done."

"Bug girl," I correct him, and he laughs, sucking down more smoke.

"Maybe that's half the problem." He blows out a white-blue breath. "Not that it stopped that mother of yours. She just won the first race at Hollywood Park."

For a half second I freeze. It's not the news that surprises me, but the casual way in which he says it. Of course, my mom is just a jockey to him. Now that she's on the West Coast, she's even less – just a typed name and an image on a screen. Now she's hardly human. Then an angry little bubble rises in my chest, snapping me out of it. There are only so many people who get to casually mention my mother, and lifers certainly aren't on that list.

"Thanks for the update," I roll my eyes. "How much did you lose on her race?"

He guffaws, putting out the cigarette, but I don't give him time to answer.

"I'm sure my dad will take your criticisms to heart, old man."

Then I walk away.

Chapter Two

The sky glows orange and rusty red when Dad pulls his SUV onto our street in Garden City. The twenty minute drive from the track and the ever dulcet tones of NPR always lull me into an exhausted coma by the time we hit Hempstead Turnpike. I cuddle into the passenger seat without caring how much dirt I'm rubbing into the leather, since the car is covered in dirt and permanently smells of horses.

When I crack my eyes open, I find my neighborhood being terrorized by kids experiencing the rush that is the first week of summer. There are mountain bikes lying on their side, deserted in the middle of the cul-de-sac. Owen and Mike, brothers from two houses down, have shucked the shirts off of their teenage boy bodies and throw a football in the middle of the street. A toss goes wild across the Jacoby family's wide lawn, the ball sailing over the SUV's nose, landing in Mrs. Cooper's award-winning front garden.

The celebration spills over onto our front yard. A group of elementary school girls sit in a small circle in the grass, whispering like they're hatching a nefarious plot. You never know. They could be planning to liberate Shady, our indoor cat, whom they taunt by plastering their foreheads against our ground floor windows until she comes over to investigate.

Cretins. Their pastel overalls don't fool me.

In the neighboring driveway, Bri Wagner sits in a lawn chair, an open book cradled in her lap. Her little sister is one of the cretins, dressed all in lavender and whispering to the girl in pink. Bri and I trade looks, eyebrows quirking upward.

Bri Wagner and I have known each other since we were two when we bonded over chalk drawings on our driveways. She doesn't entirely get the horse thing, sort of how I don't totally get why she knows *Pride and Prejudice* by heart. We were going to room together at NYU in the fall, before I let all those deadlines fly by during senior year because how can I have time for college when the track consumes my life?

"I'm surprised Bri wasn't at the race," Dad says, shocking me by speaking without being prompted. I twist away from studying the elementary school mob, unprepared to respond. Luckily he keeps talking, miracle of miracles. "When is her move-in day?"

Maybe this isn't such a miracle. I swallow, my tongue tacky and dry from the track. The smell of dirt and horses seems to fill every ounce of my being, right down to my nose and saliva. It's under my fingernails, in the creases of my skin. I force myself not to spit when I get out of the car after Dad parks in the cool garage.

"She's getting her assignment in August," I say, opening the back door and pulling out my equipment bag, hefting it up on my shoulder. "It sounds like a ton of work. Did you know you have to RSVP just to check-in? The madness must be intense."

"What's she think about doing it alone?" He holds the door open for me and snatches up Shady before she can dart for the open garage door. The cat mews plaintively, a sign that the claws will soon come out, and I scurry inside.

"She does have parents," I say, dodging the issue and speed walking into the kitchen, making a beeline to the mail my sister has stacked on the island counter. Bills. Perfect. I'll have to get to those before Dad can accidentally throw them in the trash. There will be no repeats of last time. I, for one, enjoy warm showers.

Dad puts Shady down and she leaps onto my bag, rubbing her little black body all over it and leaving a trail of hair in her wake. Dad heads into his office off the kitchen, where he normally settles in for the long haul after coming home from the track. Work has been following him home from the track since Mom left, like the more surrounded we are by horses the less likely we'll notice this gaping hole in our lives.

"You know what I mean, Juls," Dad says from the office.

I roll my eyes. We are such creatures of habit, and now we can't even confront each other normally.

"I do," I say, ripping open one of the bills. There's no sense in denying it.

"There's no animosity there?" Dad asks, the sound of the computer booting up chiming from the office. "Bri must be especially understanding, because I can't say I've ever easily forgiven people who back out on their word."

My fingers stall on the envelope, and I suck in my cheeks until I have plenty of flesh to bite down on to keep myself from blowing up. If memory serves, he's always been easy to forgive. *Too* easy to forgive, if you count how he's handled an AWOL wife and mother too busy with her career to recognize her family's existence. Dad's policy, as far as I can tell, has always been out of sight, out of mind. And Mom's been out of sight for a while. Sometimes I think he's forgotten she ever existed.

"Bri understands," I mutter at the bills. Dad grunts something unintelligible, and then he's right there in the kitchen with me, standing on the other side of the island with his hands flat on the granite. I don't look at his face, preferring to stare at his blunt fingers and the track dirt encasing them.

"I don't know what you're thinking," he says. "You have the grades, and you have the ability, and letting all those deadlines sail by is not like you, Juls. I don't think you've missed a deadline in your life, so I've got to ask you again. This time I'd like a straight answer."

"I can't," I start, jumping out of the gate like a panicked yearling. How do you describe your actions when you have no logical explanations? Anything I could say would sound like an excuse, and I know he'll call me out on it. He's done it enough when I've tried to cover for horses I've liked in the past, blaming myself for their physical failings in the morning, and Dad has always seen right past it.

"It isn't the right time," I decide to say. "Why follow up school immediately with more school? Can't I have more than one measly summer before I make that decision?"

"You had more than one summer," Dad points out. "It was called high school."

I shift uncomfortably, feeling the sweat drying between my shirt and my skin. I bend over to pick up Shady and my bag, hiking both into my arms.

"It was my decision," I say, lifting my head in an attempt to look proud. I bungle it by holding a squirming cat to my chest.

"And I'm holding you to that," Dad answers, managing cool calm far better. "I've decided that if you're not doing the college thing with Bri, you'll contribute around here like your sister."

A scoff pops out of me before I can bring it back, and Dad steamrolls right over it.

"I'll offer you the same deal I offered Martina when she left school," he says. "I'll put you on the payroll at the stable, officially, which means more horses in the mornings, more duties, and more work or you'll find some other job. You'll pay rent for your room, and you'll chip in for groceries. It's time to act like an adult, Juls. That's what you seem to want, so I expect I won't get any attitude about it."

My mouth falls open, but I quickly snap it shut.

"I choose the stable," I say shortly, and turn on my heel, stomping away from him as Martina stumbles in the front door, kicking her heels off as she goes. Her office clothes are wrinkled and her long, brown hair is gathered into a wind-blown bun. I glare at her as we pass in the hallway, and she reacts in kind.

"What?" she asks, picking up her pumps and smoothing her hair off her forehead. She's braved the subway today, and I can tell she's irritable and exhausted. I don't care.

"Thanks for setting such a great precedent for me, Martina," I say to her, letting Shady down so she can dart up the stairs and away from us. "You'll be thrilled to know I'm in your league now."

A dawning smile curls up her lips, and she says, "I'm glad you're joining the ranks, July. How are you going to make rent? Are your maid services for hire?"

"I'm working for Dad," I grumble, dropping the bag in the hall closet and opening the front door.

"Wouldn't want real life to intrude too far," she calls over her shoulder on her way up the stairs.

"It's real enough," I say to myself, stepping outside and immediately ducking when Owen's football crashes into our azaleas.

"Sorry, Juls!" comes a yell. I pick the ball up and throw it back to him on my way to Bri's driveway. She's dragged out a second lawn chair from the garage, and I collapse into it. It's only after she turns the page in her book that she marks her place and rests it gently on the pavement.

"Not good?" she asks.

"Kali's a wreck," I say, redoing my ponytail and slumping down in my seat. Mine is not the posture of the assured. "She wasn't claimed, but she didn't do anything groundbreaking either."

"Maybe she needs a break," Bri says. "Maybe you all need a break. You guys work so much you're making me feel bad about taking a vacation before college. If I had your work ethic I'd have taken classes over the summer."

"A break sounds perfect," I say, envious that Bri is going to the Outer Banks at the end of summer. "However, I was just informed that if I'm not going to college this year, it's the track for me. I'm officially on Dad's payroll. You know what that means."

"That you need to get your applications in so you can start in spring," Bri says. I let my head fall back with a groan. "Seriously," she continues, "I will help you and then we're going to the beach. You deserve it."

"You know I can't," I say. "I'm working with the horses this summer."

Bri rolls her eyes. "Come on. You work with the horses every summer. You work with the horses every day, every year, and if you're not very careful you'll work with them forever. This is the summer you need a break."

"I won't argue with that."

"So come with me," Bri insists. "It's the week before I have to move into the dorms. You'll be back from Saratoga then, and by that point you'll deserve a rest."

"Maybe," I say. "I want to, I do. It's just . . ."

"The horses," she supplies for me, knowing the reason I persist in being New York-bound.

"The horses," I echo, nodding.

Bri's acceptance of this is long-standing and legendary.

"One of these days," Bri says, "I'm going to introduce you to the joys of normal life."

"I think it's too late for me," I say. "Besides, I want to make sure I don't miss Mom."

"You don't think she's going to show up this summer," she says with a healthy dose of disbelief.

The look on my face must say it all, because she lets out her breath like a whine. "Juls, she hasn't shown up any other summer. Why this year?"

"She showed up in February," I remind her. "Who's to say she'd be able to ignore a whole summer of fantastic racing opportunities?"

"Because she's got those same opportunities in California," Bri says simply. "What does she need New York for?"

I don't answer straight away.

The part of me, the part that doesn't want to let Kali go, is beginning to flutter nervously. I'm surprised by myself, because after four years I thought I'd be more resigned to the facts. Mom left, and she's not coming back unless she has a good reason. Martina and I are not that reason, so I've got to work with what she's going to give me. I resent that about as much as her absence, and the thought makes the pit in my stomach churn. If she comes back for a horse, it will be sudden and quick, and I don't want to be in the Outer Banks at the time.

"I know that if she shows up, I don't want to miss it like I did last time."

"Juls," Bri sighs. She's one of the few people I've ever talked to about Mom, so I should probably listen to her. In fact, she's the only person I talk to because Martina is never around and Dad is an expert at avoiding the topics he doesn't want to talk about. That leaves Bri, and if ever there was a voice of reason, it is Bri. "Staying for the horses is one thing, but staying for your mom . . ."

"I know," I interrupt her, but she keeps going.

"You'd be driving yourself crazy. Don't sit around waiting for her," Bri says strongly, like she's making me promise. "She made a bad decision coming back in February."

"Yes, in the sense that her horse didn't finish the race," I say, a ball of frustration working its way into my throat. "If she had an amazing horse, she'd be back here in a heartbeat. All she does is follow horses."

"Maybe," Bri says, less urgently than before. "But you've been obsessed with her career all year. And even though I keep pointing out how unhealthy that is, you keep getting better at it. You probably know more about her daily schedule than she does, so how could she possibly get past you?"

I shoot a watery smile over at her. "You've got a point."

"Precisely," she says. "So give me some hope on the vacation front?"

"Okay," I say. My eyes are raw, despite the fact that I haven't cried. I haven't cried over Mom in a long time, because I refuse. "Maybe."

"I'm going to hold you to that," Bri says smartly.

A football sails out of the sky and lands inches from the cretins, scattering them with shrieks and grass stains. It makes an awkward bounce and heads right at Bri, who snatches it expertly and stands up.

"Owen!" she shouts, throwing it back at him as he comes loping up to catch it. "Stick with baseball, would you? There's a reason you never played football in high school."

"Come on, you two," he says with his most winning smile, sauntering up to Bri and wrapping an arm around her waist. He swings her up, twirling them onto the grass. "It's summer. Poorly play catch with us."

Bri wiggles out of his grip, straightening her crisp white tunic and brushing her hands over her pink skinny jeans. She looks down at her ballet flats, and then at my clunky riding boots.

"What do you think?" she asks me. "Want to teach these boys how to aim?"

I shrug. "I guess I can squeeze a lesson in," I say, standing up and darting around Owen, stealing the football from his loose grip. Bri laughs and takes off into the street as I twist around and throw, the ball arcing up and falling into her hands.

We go until dusk, running plays no one has ever heard of and dashing down the street with the ball flying through the air. The boys are panting when we're done, and Bri stands triumphant in her front yard with the ball tucked under her arm.

"Winner and still champion!" she yells, lifting the ball over her head. Owen tackles her and they fall laughing to the grass. I roll my eyes and step over them, announcing my retirement from the game.

Bri shoves Owen onto his back and sits up, bits of grass in her tumbling brown hair. "Remember what I said, July!"

"Maybe vacation!" I yell over my shoulder, waving goodbye as I walk into the house and climb the stairs. I feel a little guilty, because I know there will be no time. Vacations in my family are rare events squeezed between races. I can count them on one hand, and even those amount to only a few hours each. Shopping in Los Angeles. Sinking my toes into snow white sand in Florida. They are tiny slips of memory strung around horses.

I meet Shady at the door to my bedroom, where she's pawing at it in a hopeless attempt to get in without my help. Shady leaps onto my bed and flops down, rolling across the unmade sheets. I pull off my boots and stalk over to my desk. When I open up my laptop, my e-mail glows on the screen where I left it. I glance over the new messages as I yank off my socks and throw them in the direction of my boots.

The room is a wreck, but unlike the stable or most of the house, I feel compelled to leave it this way. The area rug on the hardwood floor is askew. Shady uses the bedding as a slide from the mattress to the floor. There are half-read books sitting in small piles on every flat surface so my bookshelves can hold all my horse figurines. The dusky blue walls look cheerful under the old photos I've hammered into the plaster; win photos, horse photos, pictures of Bri and me going back ages. The frames are so old the photos stick to the glass, which I discovered the second I tried to make any changes. So things don't change. I'm more than okay with that.

My eyes fall on the photo I keep next to my computer. From the frame, images of me, Martina, and Mom smile wide, showing all of our teeth. I'm barely ten, and Martina is in her rangy teen phase. Almost beautiful, but angular and bony, like a yearling caught in a growth spurt. Mom's deep brown hair falls in wild waves around her shoulders, her pointed nose crinkled and sharp with her smile. She's squinting, her eyes dark slits crossing her face. Her arms fold around us and the horse that inserts himself in the photo, one big brown head that presents itself right before the shutter snaps.

The horse is Dad's wiry gelding, Pluck, second-place finisher in the Kentucky Derby and the best horse Dad's ever had. His long neck wraps around all three of us from behind, like he could keep us tethered together. The poor guy had his work cut out for him.

I scroll through my e-mail, opening up a message with the subject line *Jockey Notification Message*.

With a quick scroll of the mouse, my mother's name appears in big blue letters.

Celia Carter.

Her entries follow. June 28, June 29, July 1. She's at Hollywood Park now, racing until mid-July. Then where? Del Mar, in San Diego, until September. Then back to Santa Anita all the way through April. It's a routine I know as well as she does, but the problem has always been that I can't account for her spur of the moment decisions. I can't know when a trainer calls her the day before a race and asks her to ride.

Even the Internet can't help me, with its spontaneous updates and e-mails. I can't know where she'll be next week, not really, but this is the next best thing to knowing for sure.

I schedule each of her rides into my phone, turning my calendar into a running log of Celia Carter's races one by one. Tracks, times, horses, and trainers mesh together and offer a prediction of where she'll be next. If a trainer she rides for has a big horse in New York, the more likely she might show up at Belmont or Saratoga or Aqueduct unannounced.

On the computer, Mom's results flash up at me like a tease, beckoning me to watch the videos. I have so many of them already, saved on my computer and scratchy on barely salvageable video tape. There are stacks of DVDs in my room all with her name scrawled across them in different colors of Sharpie, dates and races in tiny print to keep them all straight.

I hover the mouse over a $40,000 maiden claiming race, just like the one we had Kali in today. It's a race filled with expensive losers, one of which was lucky enough to have my mom on board.

I click the link, and the room is filled with track noise. The announcer's crackly voice ekes out of the laptop's tiny speakers, and the screen fills with an image of Hollywood Park's white and green starting gate and the horses that file inside of it. I can't tell where she is straight away, but when the horses leap onto the track and spread out, I spot her on a giant bay, some of her long hair spilling out of her helmet and ripping like a horse tail behind her.

The gelding takes the narrow path down the inside, slipping between the leader and glancing off the rail, his huge hindquarters bunching and working. Mom hunches over his withers and throws her arms up his neck, reins swinging and crop flipping up into her fingers to come down in one swift slap on his darkening coat.

Mom pushes harder, and the gelding pins his ears, listening to her and delivering more than he's probably ever given in his life. She doesn't let him stop until he's under the wire a half-length in front. Only then does she ease up on his neck to let him know.

That's enough now.

She pats his neck and he arches into her hold, galloping so front heavy I think only Mom's arms keep him from toppling into the dirt. They slow and slow until they stop, and Mom sits back down in the saddle, scrubbing her fingers up and down the gelding's mane.

Then the screen goes black and I'm left with my quiet room, surrounded by her and completely alone.

Chapter Three

Horses in training arrive on the track at five thirty every morning. I am usually exercising the racers, but if Dad has other plans I'm always nearby on Maggie, my Paint pace horse that may have never seen a race, but can keep up with most racers on a good day.

Today is one of those "other plans" days. Maggie stands like a rock underneath me, totally trustworthy, and I swing a leather lead from my fingers as I wait for Gus to bring Lamplighter down from 27. Most of the works are finished, but we've saved Lighter for the end of the day, because he's a hellion and he knows it.

A loud bang makes my normally sturdy mare jump, and I have to reel her in before she swings around to bolt. The mare does a full circle, coming to a perplexed stop until she sees what's coming at her. It's only Lighter, with Gus clinging to the colt's bridle and Pilar folded on his back. Maggie tugs on the reins, taking a couple of steps forward. I sink my weight down, bringing Maggie to an instant halt.

Lighter is a two-year-old time bomb, built to move and move fast, but mentally capable of doing little more than cause trouble and scream for more food. I wasn't much impressed with him when he arrived at the barn, and I have only steadily become exasperated with him since. I suppose he's pretty. That coppery chestnut coat and oddball flaxen mane and tail would have won him a beauty contest if manners weren't a factor.

With me, manners are always a factor. Lighter fails in this department routinely. I'm lucky I'm not the one to ride him today, because this morning Mr. Lighter woke up with a new zeal for life. This can't be a good sign.

Right at that moment, the colt goes up in the air, ripping right out of Gus's grip and sending Pilar up on his neck. I tense on Maggie's back, and the mare takes that as a sign to move, otherwise the colt is going to land right on top of us and I know I don't want to be sandwiched between two half-ton, struggling animals. Maggie and I dart to the side, and Lighter comes back down to earth with Pilar still situated on the colt's back and a grin on her face. Her left hand is firmly rooted in Lighter's mane, the other strangling the reins.

Gus reaches one fully tattooed arm out to snag Lighter's head and calls the colt all sorts of names in Spanish. Lighter tries to fling his head up, but Gus holds on like a bulldog until Lighter stands still. Being Lighter's groom is death defying, but Gus handles it with a practiced ease. I can't help smiling, which is how most people respond to Gus no matter what. He's in his late twenties, dark and gorgeous. I would dare anyone to not smile like an idiot around him.

"You okay?" he checks on Pilar, who rolls her eyes.

"Please," she says, like she's been offended. A few long strands of curly black hair stick out of her helmet over her forehead, and she pushes them aside. "Get back to me when he dumps my ass on the track."

Gus grunts at that, unimpressed with her bravado. Pilar wouldn't show if she was shaken up anyway, and what's a little rearing around a racetrack?

I lean over and slip the lead through Lighter's bridle, apprehensive because I've now attached myself to a mentally deficient wild thing. Gus gives Lighter a pat on his bronze neck, decides this is the perfect time to spit over his heavily muscled shoulder onto the gravel, and leaves me to it.

"So I hear you're officially one of us," Pilar says to me with a knowing look. She flicks her long black braid behind her and rubs a sweaty hand over the worn denim that stretches over her knees.

"Not that I wasn't before." I nudge Maggie forward, chauffeuring Lighter and Pilar to the training track. "I just get to give half my paycheck back to Dad at the end of the day instead."

Pilar makes a face and reaches over to thwack me on the thigh with her crop.

"Hey!" I push her back with my mare, since I'm out of crops to retaliate with. There's no point when I'm riding Maggie. "What was that for?"

"I don't want to hear about your crap paycheck," Pilar says. "You know the rules."

"Yeah, yeah," I groan. "We've all got crap paychecks."

Pilar may be a jockey, but she's still scrounging for mounts and picking up rides in the mornings. She started out exercising for us two years ago when she was sixteen, and got her jockey's license after Dad encouraged her. Pilar is simply too good to waste on morning rides. The pay, of course, still mostly sucks.

Lighter shoves his nose over Maggie's withers. His blond head nudges into my lap, ears flicking every which way and one brown eye rolling up at me like he's plotting something childish in his pea-sized brain. Maggie keeps her ears back, monitoring her charge with the patience of an overworked but extremely professional nanny. I'm keeping my eye on him, too. Right up there with not wanting him to rear and land on me is not wanting him to toss his head and catch me in the face.

"Besides," Pilar says, running her fingers down Lighter's pale mane. "Don't act like you haven't got any options. I know all about your great deadline debacle."

"The backside gossip network strikes again." I give Maggie a nudge, and she shoulders into Lighter, who still refuses to remove his head from my lap. "Does everyone think I'm a complete moron?"

Pilar shakes her head. "Of course not. You're talking about people who choose to be here, July. We've got our reasons, and I suspect you have yours."

I press my lips together and look out at the view of the track emerging from between the barns. It sweeps by in a wide arc, bobbing horses and riders dotting the surface and the grandstand stretching out in a swath of green behind them all.

Pilar sings a few Spanish stanzas, which makes Lighter bob his head. He gives Maggie a little more room to breathe. A shameful wash of relief sweeps over me, simply because I know the conversation will shift to the track. I won't have to talk about how college feels impossible, horseless in a world where all I know is horses and admit my fear.

"He's like a toddler," Pilar says, letting me off the hook. "If you can distract him he's a happy boy."

"He's a happy boy because he's got the attention span of a gnat," I say. "A toddler might not be too far off base."

Pilar scoffs, disappointed in me. "He's a baby, July. It's expected. Besides, one day that attitude of yours will change and boys like this one will be a joy to work with."

"Unlikely," I say, because it really is.

"You know we're taking Lighter to Saratoga," Pilar says, and I blanch.

"Who said that?"

"Your dad."

I groan, because this is not Dad's idea. That has to be Lighter's owner's doing. I would throttle him if I knew where he was. There's no anticipating Beckett Delaney, mainly because he tends to show up unannounced at the least convenient of times. He treats 27 like a very shoddy, unkempt second home. I would fume about it, but I can't because the guy is Laurence Delaney's son, and Laurence Delaney owns Blackbridge Farm, Dad's employer.

Fine. So Beck does technically own Barn 27. I may be deluding myself.

"We'll see about that," I mutter under my breath.

Lighter is not ready for Saratoga. That Dad said yes to this means he gave in to Beck's pestering.

We hit the track and head down the backstretch. The training track is a mile long, a full half mile less than the famous main track. Considering Lighter's age he's only doing a three furlong breeze by himself. We canter down the middle of the backstretch, Lighter's head still craned over Maggie's neck, the mare's ears lying back flat. When we approach the start of the breeze I undo the lead.

The colt is off like a shot, a good few strides before the marker. Maggie and I veer off to the outside rail and mosey down to a halt. I watch Lighter flatten out going into the bend, his blond mane and tail flickering like white flame. I turn Maggie, headed back the way we came at a brisk trot so we're ready to catch them in their cool down.

This, however, would be asking too much. Naturally Lighter has to throw a kink into the works, because I'm cantering down the track when the PA system crackles to life.

Loose horse.

Across the infield is Lighter, his head up, ears up, reins flapping wildly around his neck. Pilar is certainly not on his back. I glance further down the track and see her sitting in the dirt, shoving herself to her feet. I don't have much time to dwell on Pilar's condition because Lighter gallivants into the first turn, shying around any outrider attempting to catch him.

Maggie huffs eagerly at the action; this is where she's particularly skilled. I would really like to see Lighter try to get away from her, because I'm sure my mare could kick his ass on any given day.

I turn Maggie around and wait for him to speed up on my inside. The mare champs at the bit, rocking from her hind feet to her front legs like a crazy rocking horse. I urge Maggie into action before Lighter sprints by. The mare lunges like she's coming out of the starting gate, and I reach down to grip the horn on the saddle.

Lighter realizes a challenge when he sees one. You have to admire that in the colt—he likes competition. Maggie has him, though, and a few strides go by before I stretch out and grab his reins. Lighter gives me the evil eye and does the last thing I ever expected. He throws on the brakes.

I don't let go of his reins. I should have. My arm wrenches back, quickly followed by my whole torso, followed by my body. Maggie throws her head up at the accidental pressure this puts on her bit, and just like that I'm airborne.

I let go of both horses midair, and two seconds later I make impact with the ground. Pain blooms from my shoulder all the way down my back. Lighter goes thundering by me, gleefully zigzagging up and down the track. I can see the little jerk from where I'm stationed in the dirt, flat on my back and trying to find some breath. It comes swiftly back into my lungs, which burn like fire, and it takes me a moment to summon the willpower to sit up.

Maggie waits next to me, her head down with a baleful expression on her face, like this is all her fault.

"It's not, girl," I reassure her, and take a minute to stand. I don't want to get all the way onto two feet and then crumple because my legs can't hold me. They're shaky right now.

"Juls," Dad says as he walks toward me across the track. He got here quickly from where he usually stands for the works. "Do you need an ambulance?"

"Just got the wind knocked out of me," I say, noticing that another outrider has caught the wretched colt, who is swinging his hindquarters around like a dancer. I can see the whites of his eyes from here. I am glad to note that the outrider is a burly man, who can probably muscle Lighter around. Then I think about this more and it makes me much less pleased with myself.

"I'm fine." I stand up and walk unsteadily to Maggie, getting ready to jump back on before Dad catches my arm and pulls me to face him.

"That was some fall," he says, and I definitely know this. I was lucky that Lighter decided not to trample me while he was at it. "Why don't you go up to the barn and take a break."

"A break," I say slowly, like I'm trying out foreign words that have no meaning to me.

"We're almost done here," Dad says. "Last two horses are already on their way down. Go cool off Maggie."

I don't know what to say to this, because this sounds like fatherly behavior. Usually he gives me a leg up into the saddle, pats me on the knee, and says something inane like "good work" or "take it easy" before he's hiking back to the clocker's stand.

"Yeah," I say, wincing as I turn back to Maggie. "Sure."

He gives me a leg up into the saddle, pats my knee, and says, "Good try, Juls."

All is right with the world.

~∽

By late afternoon, my jeans are damp and dragging on my legs. My pale pink tank top is stained an earthy dust hue, and there's enough dirt caked under my nails to make me look homeless. I wipe the sweat off the back of my neck as I walk down the barn aisle, looking in on our horses and rubbing the noses of those that aren't tempted to take a piece out of me as I pass.

Galaxy Collision, our undefeated wonder filly, gets her routine peppermint and a scratch on the forehead. She tickles my fingers with her mouth and swings her head away when I don't offer any more sweets. Next to her is Quark Star, our best-kept secret who is set to run in the Dwyer Stakes next week. The big dark colt tosses his head up and down, flinging his nearly black mane off his neck. I put my hand on his forehead and he quiets, giving me a soft stare. I stare right back, rub between his eyes and manage a well-placed kiss on his nose while he's standing still.

My true love, besides my ever-present Maggie, is Diver. I slip up to his stall and stick my head in, greeted only by his broad, light gray rump.

"Hey, bud," I say to get his attention and he cocks an ear back, turning his head from the important task of ripping his hay net to shreds. Faced with the prospect of getting attention, he maneuvers himself around so he can butt his head against my chest, insisting rather than asking for me to scratch him everywhere. I comply, working my short nails over his coat.

At eight, Diver is the oldest racer in the barn. There are plenty of old photos stashed away in my room where Diver and Mom stand grass-stained and exhausted in the winner's circle. The two were a force of nature once, raking up purse money and putting Mom's name up there with some of the best female jockeys in the world. No one connected with him like Mom on the racetrack, and although Diver is still just as good as he always was, there's a spark missing from his races. Call me crazy, but I think he used to love racing. Now it's a job.

Sometimes I think Diver was just as confused as the rest of us when Mom disappeared.

Who knows when Diver will call it quits, but I've been clear with Laurence Delaney that I want him when he's retired. This is only possible because Diver's a gelding, and his future isn't set in stone. I've asked, and asked, and asked some more. Delaney has said maybe, maybe, and maybe again and again.

"You could be my new pace horse when Maggie retires," I tell him when an infinitely better idea hits me. "Or I could take you to Woodfield," the thought of my old lesson barn stretching a smile on my lips. "You could be a dressage horse easy, right?"

Diver knocks his hoof against the side of his stall, shoving his nose into me and pulling back to see if my shirt might be tasty. I shift out of the way and stroke my hand down his face. He bats his big brown eyes and I smile up at him.

He's the perfect horse, sweet and willing. He'd climb into your lap if he didn't weigh half a ton, and sometimes that doesn't stop him from trying. I can already see myself on him without the exercise saddle and the black shadow roll Dad always wants affixed to his noseband. I take a deep breath, feeling peaceful here in the nook by Diver's stall.

And then it's shattered.

"Hey, kiddo."

I would like to point out that Beck Delaney is precisely ten months older than me. I don't know why he persists in treating me like I'm a ten-year-old tomboy. I may be the latter part of that combination, but I've surpassed kid status by now.

I haven't seen Beck in a few months, but he hasn't changed. His brown hair, which was blond once upon a time, is still a ragged sort of short. There's enough of it to mess up if he ran his hands through it. I have to look up at him, because he's been a good six feet tall since a couple of years ago. He rests against the stall's doorframe in a plain white T-shirt and beat up jeans, that mischievousness glowing around the edges. There's something in his hazel eyes that sparks. It makes me uneasy. Like his horse, Beck is almost always plotting something ridiculous.

It feels like I've known Beck forever, and during that time I've mostly been exasperated. Beck turned my hair purple for a week when I was twelve. He put curlers in Maggie's mane overnight and painted her hooves pink when I was thirteen. Mayonnaise filled donuts when I was fourteen. Then there was the time he filled my car with packing peanuts the first day I drove it to Saratoga. Pranks have never been my forte, so I make up for it by retaliating with my scathing wit. But that was then.

Now Beck's around far less, busy with freshman year at Columbia.

"You're a whole day late. Just about right for you," I say, ducking into Diver's stall in a heroic attempt to act like Beck's presence isn't all that important.

"Late for what?" Beck asks, his eyes flicking from the gelding to me.

I tug at the base of Diver's mane, which has always sat askew on his neck and has always bothered me. I decide to fix that instead of giving Beck the attention he wants, focusing on the task of braiding the strands in an effort to train it to lay on the other side of Diver's neck. Beck's shadow falls right across my face, and I frown at the braid that I work between my fingers.

"For Kali's race," I say, looking up when I get no response. Nothing like recognition registers on his face.

"Your dad owns her," I supply, implying he's a complete dumbass for not knowing this. "Kaliningrad. Chestnut filly, white socks, ran yesterday . . ."

He still seems to have no clue and I sigh. Typical.

"Never mind."

I don't know why I keep expecting him to know as much about Blackbridge as anyone else in the stable, including Beck's dad, the great Lawrence Delaney himself. Beck only sometimes shows up on big race days. He's here for Lighter, possibly. Every so often he likes to show off the colt, as if Lighter is going to win next year's Kentucky Derby, which I can say with absolute certainty he will not.

"So why are you here?" I ask. I finish Diver's braid, smoothing it against his neck.

Beck smiles at me, this stupid lopsided smile that tells me a whole lot about what he's here for and what he knows. "Lighter," he says, and settles his back against the stall's opening like he's going to be here for a while. "Your dad called me about his adventure this morning. You okay?"

I glower at him silently for a moment. "It was just a fall," I say, irritated that Dad decided to tell Beck of all people that Lighter got the better of me today. "They happen occasionally."

"I've gathered he's a handful."

"That's an understatement," I say, amused that he's acting like he just now noticed this. Beck's known about Lighter's issues since he bought him at auction last year as a birthday present to himself. According to him, the colt had knocked over his handler in the auction ring. From what I can gather, this was one of the main reasons Beck bought him. And he was cheap. "A steal," Beck had said at the time. "It was like they were giving him away. And how could I turn down this face?"

At the time he said that, Lighter was giving Gus a look that I've come to associate with *watch out*. Two seconds later, Lighter had a hunk of sleeve in his mouth, ripped right off the rest of Gus's shirt.

"Oh, come on, Juls," Beck says as I duck under Diver's stall guard and back into the aisle. "You know you love him."

"Just like I love being yanked off a horse at a dead gallop," I say. "It's definitely fabulous. You should try it."

"Okay," he shrugs, lifting himself off the wall and easing into my personal space. Just enough, because he knows I don't like it. He wouldn't be Beck if he wasn't always trying to see what he can get away with. "I'll apologize for my horse."

"Are you kidding?" I ask.

"Come on, Juls," he says. "I'm genuinely sorry Lighter's kind of an asshole. But you know he's worth it in the long run."

"No, I don't."

"Sure you do," Beck says. "At Saratoga . . ."

"Which reminds me," I interrupt him, and he falls silent, wincing and backing up a step. "I want you to know you're insane."

"Brilliant insane, or hopeless psychotic insane?"

"Definitely not the first option," I say.

"I don't think it's that big of a deal. I want him to start running next month, not when Belmont opens in September. Your dad agrees, and that's why we're taking Lighter to the farm this summer. I know you'd rather take a Lighter break, but you ride Star most mornings and I know he's more of a pain in the ass than Lighter. Star is going to Saratoga."

"Star is just full of himself."

"And Lighter isn't?"

"Star is worth my time."

"Lighter will be," he says, so assured. No wonder he's so good at talking people into things. It's a gift that Beck is definitely using for pure deviousness. "Come on, July. I'm starting to think you don't like my horse, and that isn't like you."

Okay, so it isn't like me.

"I don't dislike him," I say, covering my bases. "I just don't think he's ready yet."

"Ah," he says, that spark in him flaring. "But that's my call to make."

"Then it will be a wrong one," I say cheerfully. He gives me a smirk, because this is where the conversation is going to end. I can protest all I like, but Beck owns the horse. What he wants goes. I may be the only one that sees any sense, but that doesn't mean I'll automatically get my way. Even if I have Dad on my side, Lighter would still come with us to Saratoga.

I'll have to get ready for more falls this summer. I'll be lucky if I don't break something, although the prospect of blaming Beck for any serious injuries does make it less awful.

"Then how about a bet," he says, and I don't say anything because this ought to be interesting. "If he finishes up the track in this first race, I'll concede to you the wrongness of my decision. If he finishes third or better, I want to see you work him every morning he goes to the track, unless your dad says otherwise."

I shake my head, because this is horrible. "Third or better is too generous," I say. "He'd have to win. And if he finishes up the track, you admitting you were wrong isn't worth it."

"Have I ever admitted I've been wrong?" he asks, and I have to think about that one, because I can't remember a time. I remember a lot of apologies, but never any admission of wrongdoing. Usually he follows up an apology with an immediate *but*. Kind of like, *"I'm sorry my horse is kind of an asshole, but you know he's worth it."*

"Regardless," I say, crossing my arms and shifting my weight to one leg. "He wins, or goes back to Belmont."

"That's not going to happen," he says, sighing like he'd really like to make this bet happen, if only I'd negotiate.

"How about this," I say, brightening. He squirms nervously at my sudden smile. "He wins, or you work him the rest of the meet."

"Your dad will never go for that."

"You can ride as well as I can," I say, and his expression turns to horror. "Maybe you're a little rusty . . ."

"A little rusty?" he asks. "July, I haven't ridden on the track in two years."

"Then you'll have to brush up on it," I tell him. "It's like riding a bike."

"No it isn't," he says seriously.

"You can practice on Maggie. And Diver is a good sport, you can graduate up to him when you're ready."

"I cannot believe this," he says. "Your dad won't go for this at all, and because of that I'll agree."

Not that I think any of this is actually likely, but I happen to know that Dad won't really care. Beck knows how to ride as well as any exercise rider we've got. Dad will see an extra rider at his disposal, and Beck won't just eat his words, but experience the wrongness of them first hand. I smile wide, and offer my hand. He folds his hand around mine, and we shake on it.

Chapter Four

Pilar's bark of laughter can be heard down the shedrow when I tell her about the bet.

"Oh, that's perfect," she crows, throwing back a swallow of root beer from a frosty brown bottle. Her hair is undone from its braid, curling in a frizzy mane around her face and bobbing enthusiastically in time with her laughter. "So chances are if Lighter doesn't kill me this summer, Beck Delaney will have the honor."

"He's not *that bad* of a rider," I say, sniffing as I look at my cards and push the required chips in to stay in the game.

Pilar snorts, tossing in her chips. "When he was younger, lighter, and more interested, I might give you that. Not so much now. Remember when he used to play cards with us that one summer?"

"Two years ago," I say, remembering how much money I lost. When Beck found out about Friday night poker, I'd had to up my game to keep even a percentage of my earnings from my morning rides. Thankfully that only lasted a summer, and then he was gone.

"That was the summer he was a good rider," Pilar says. "Then he quit and who knows what that boy's been up to since."

"Your old man will never let it happen," Gus speaks up from his perch on the sagging old sofa in Dad's office. He leans forward to deal out the flop, during which Izzie visibly brightens. Pilar groans and throws her cards down in disgust.

"Sure," I agree. "My dad can call the whole thing off. It really all depends on how sadistic he's feeling when I tell him about it."

"Or how distracted," Izzie points out, raising the bet and forcing me out. I toss my cards face down on the battered coffee table.

"I fold," I announce, and then nod at Izzie. "You're right. He might just refuse to hear me and then I'll have potentially killed Pilar when Beck Delaney goes on a joyride with Lighter."

"Just call the whole thing off," Pilar says, folding as well and leaving it up to Gus and Izzie, who mock glare at each other. "Besides, have you taken into account that the colt might win?"

"I have every confidence he's going to lose," I say, propping my feet on the table and leaning back in the overstuffed easy chair.

Pilar shakes her head at me from her spot on the floor, thin legs crossed underneath her.

"Such confidence," she teases, swatting at my feet until I put them down on the floor. "And what will you do if he wins?"

"Bri invited me to the beach this summer," I say, shrugging. "If Lighter wins his maiden then it might be a perfect time for me to go."

"And abandon us?" Izzie asks with a gasp, calling and throwing down her cards. Pilar and I stretch to see the results as Izzie cheerfully scoops up her winnings and Gus flops over on the sofa, groaning into the cushions.

"Stop being such a baby," Izzie says, smacking Gus on the thigh and pushing the cards my way. "It's July's turn to deal."

I arrange the cards back into an orderly deck, tapping them against the table.

"I'd never abandon you, Izzie," I tell her, and she blows me a kiss over her freshly painted purple nails.

In the morning, the sun is already high in the sky when I finish the day's works with Diver. It's only a couple of hours away from post time for the first race of the day. Diver's coat shimmers with dapples as we walk underneath the line of trees on our way back from the practice track. No one escorts Diver, so it's just us moseying back to the barn. It's a perfect time to experiment.

Diver tips his ears back as I nudge him into shoulder fore, just to see if he'll do it for me. He does, reaching underneath himself and trotting down the rail like a horse on a mission, like he hasn't galloped two miles flat. It's perfect, everything between us clicking into place. It's almost better than feeling him *go*, running forty miles an hour like the devil is on his tail.

I straighten him out and give him a pat. He drops into a walk with a sigh and I pull my feet from the stirrups, taking our time. I rock along with the plodding four-beat of Diver's walk, listening to the clop and scrape of his hooves on the gravel, all the while whispering Mom's age-old advice to myself: *move with the rhythm*.

When Diver drops his nose, mouthing the bit, I think *encourage, drive*. Diver extends his stride and bobs his head. I nudge him once and he lifts up into an airy trot, flicking his ears back at me uncertainly, as if saying *is this what you want?*

Yes.

I ease back in the saddle, collecting him and asking for more. My body says *go, but come back to me. Look for me.* Instead of spitting out the bit in confusion, Diver shortens his stride, suspends each foot a fraction longer than he normally would, and floats up to 27. A smile spreads over my face, the pure thrill of coming together with the horse underneath me lighting along every nerve ending in my fingers that hold the reins, keeping the circuit buzzing from Diver to me.

Gus is waiting for me outside the barn, a toothpick perched between his front teeth. He smiles, rolls the toothpick to the corner of his lips, and says, "Getting fancy with my boy won't win races, Juls."

"Diver doesn't need my help to win races," I say, vaulting to the ground while Gus takes the gray. "Where is everyone?"

It is strangely quiet around the barn, which should be hopping after the works.

"You took too long dancing with Diver," Gus teases, leading the gelding into the shade of the shedrow. "Your old man is in the office. He's got a meeting with the idiot box."

"He's what?" I ask, but Gus has already led Diver back to the hose for a bath. I turn on my heel and head for the office, peeking inside when I see how many people have crammed themselves in Dad's tiny hole in the wall. It seems we've got most of our staff wedged inside, plus Beck. I don't even pretend to hide the double take I make at his presence. He shoots me a raised eyebrow and manages to cut through the chaos to stand by me.

"What's going on?" I ask, looking for Dad in the crowd. I spot him sitting on the edge of his desk, too busy for me to ask him what he thought of Diver, because he's pressing his cell phone rather hard to his head and is watching the television with a strangely dispassionate expression.

"Wall Street is melting down again," Beck says dryly. "Everyone's rushing to count their pennies, but it looks like they're all gone."

I suck in a deep breath and watch the television as intently as Dad. Living in New York, usually working for embarrassingly wealthy people, the backside of a track turns wild-eyed at any mention of the recent chaos on the stock market. The television helpfully informs me that this is the thirteenth Ponzi scheme to come to light this year.

The guy they show, the perpetrator, is nothing more than an average man who works in a bank. The newscaster starts to go into what all the police have found in his Manhattan apartment. Jewelry, shiny gemstones, probably too many shoes for his wife.

"Who really needs thirty-four watches?" I say to no one in particular.

"Daylight savings time must be a bitch," Beck says, and I cast an amused smirk at him over my shoulder. He's not grinning back. His face is perfectly sculpted into careful disinterest, so my smile dies and I turn back to the television.

"Yeah, okay," Dad says into his cell phone. "Keep me informed."

Then he turns off the television and yells at everyone to get back to work.

That night I don't sleep at all. Instead I study the ceiling, listening to the night noises through the open windows, wishing for sleep and failing miserably. The only thing I can think about is Beck's uneasy presence in my father's office earlier in the morning, and I can't help connecting the dots faster than I can make sense of them. The Delaney's didn't earn their wealth in horse racing, I knew that. We were pure entertainment, sponsored by Wall Street and careful investments. We were a rich man's gambling addiction.

I have to stop myself from coming to false conclusions, otherwise I'll never wake up in time for the works in the morning. I close my eyes tightly, wishing for sleep only to hear Martina come in. I hear giggling and the thump of her high heels catching on the stairs, followed by the quieter sounds of another set of footsteps.

I sigh and roll onto my stomach, burying my face in my pillow while Martina and her boyfriend of seven months, Scott, try to pad quietly down the hallway. Scott is halfway succeeding, but Martina should have taken off her shoes.

Sometimes it's hard to believe Martina is my sister. She's everything I'm not, right down to the gorgeous long dark hair and the self-righteous attitude. She's assured in everything, even arguing her way effectively into never having to clean the bathroom. I don't know how she does it, and more importantly, I don't know why I keep letting her get away with it.

I roll over again, because my shoulder still aches from my run in with Lighter and sleeping on it any way is the wrong way. The sound of Martina's door clicking closed can be heard all the way down the hallway. She was at least fortunate to have the corner room. Dad's room is the only one downstairs, sequestered away by the office, so whatever Martina does is never in his line of vision.

Breaking down, I swing my feet out from under the covers and pad quickly across to my door and head to the hallway bathroom. There's always a stash of Ibuprofen in the cabinet.

I glance at the clock on my way back to bed, realizing that tomorrow has been here for a while and technically I have an hour to sleep. Unfortunately for me, the second my head hits the pillow I'm restlessly staring at the ceiling again. Thankfully I can't hear whatever it is Martina and Scott are up to down the hallway. This is a small thing to be thankful for when I have to sleep.

After a few minutes, I give up and turn on the light, giving in to the one thing that will surely knock me out cold. I reach under my bed and hunt for the thick scrapbook that I keep not-so-secretly hidden underneath. I haul it out, my abused muscles straining at the heavy weight of the book, and open it up on the rumpled disaster of my bed covers.

On the first page is a smiling photo of Mom. We're at Saratoga in this photo. I am barely twelve, with freckles and hideous braces. Martina's hiding behind a huge pair of sunglasses too big for her face, a smile quirking on thin lips. Mom is in her Blackbridge silks, and I realize how late in the game this photo was taken. She was probably already thinking about leaving for California. Who am I kidding? She probably already had one foot out the door.

Nevertheless, we're all smiling like not a thing is wrong. I run my fingers over our faces, our similar, sharp features. Then I skip through the book, which documents a relentless effort over four years to keep up with my mother. It's all here in front of me, a history I should have seen first-hand. Instead I have it all bound together and held with so much glue stick. Clippings, race programs, photographs, winning and losing tickets, a whole life reconstructed in ink.

It makes me tired just thinking about it.

When I get to the last documented page, the piece of paper I tore out of the Aqueduct program on that miserable day in February, I stop and stare. I run my fingers over her name listed there for the Whirlaway Stakes, and I wonder when she'll come back. I wonder if there will even be a next time.

I wonder why I didn't try harder to find her that day, or if I even wanted to find her at all. All I really knew that day was running, the searing cold air in my lungs, and the nauseating rush of adrenaline over the slow realization that I'd missed my window.

I'd missed Mom. She was here so many short months ago, within my reach while I'd let her slip through my fingers. Who knew when I'd get such a chance again?

Who knew if there would be a chance at all?

∿∿

The day of the Dwyer Stakes dawns hot, humid and hellish. It's one of those big Saturdays, and we've got four horses running. Of those four, three are allowance runners, horses that run a step below the stakes. Allowance horses are the meat and potatoes of racing, running for substantial purses that don't come with trophies and blankets of flowers.

Up until today, Star was an allowance runner. As a two-year-old, he'd been too big, too gangly, too immature. Dad didn't even bother starting him until this spring, when Star seemed to finally understand how to move all four of his long legs. Last month he demolished his allowance peers, so now it's time to see what else he can do.

After today, the Belmont summer meet will wind down. If Star shows promise here, we'll take him to New Jersey for

Monmouth next to race in the Haskell, right before the big event of the season—Saratoga.

When I get my hands on one of the programs, I thumb through the pages and study every entry, scanning for Celia Carter. Beck walks by, finally appearing like he's there for more than lounging around the backside. He's upgraded his jeans and tee with a sports jacket. Aviator sunglasses mirror across his eyes. He stops to rest his chin on my shoulder, watching my rapid page flipping.

"Is this some OCD issue someone failed to acknowledge?"

"No," I say pointedly. "I just like to be informed."

Whatever truth there is to his reaction is hidden by his sunglasses. He knows I'm lying.

"That doesn't look like research to me."

"Well, you don't know me that well." I slip out from under his chin.

"I've known you since you were twelve," he calls after me. "I dare you to name one person who knows you better."

"Bri Wagner's known me since I was two. She's got ten years on you, Beck."

"I don't think she counts."

"You would think that," I say and he finally grins while I walk back into 27.

I leave it at that, walking into the shedrow. He doesn't follow me, and I assume I've won. I duck into Diver's stall and lean against the wall. The gelding nudges my shoulder in hello, and goes back to his hay with a swish of conditioned tail as I page back to the spot I left off before Beck's interruption. Then I continue to sort through the horses, looking at every jockey and making sure my mom's name isn't listed next to any horse.

The thing is, of course, that I know she isn't here today. She's in California. I know Celia Carter isn't going to pop up on any of these pages, but I keep thumbing through just to be sure. Doubly sure. I can't be surprised again. When I'm finished, she's nowhere to be seen and my fingertips are stained dark gray from all the searching.

The announcement for the fourth race, our first race for the day, echoes down the shedrow. I close the program and push away from the wall to go change in Dad's office bathroom, giving Diver a kiss on the cheek as I go. Occasionally, I can get by with jeans and a nice top for weekday races. On weekends, you can forget that. For graded races, it's a dress and heels or I sit it all out by standing at the rail with the masses. This has proven to be my undoing time and time again.

This is where Bri is a lifesaver. She started out handpicking dresses for me, and this turned into full-fledged lessons on what to wear. Unlike previously, when I required serious assistance from Martina, who used to care about these things. Martina won't show up today, so it's all up to me.

I wiggle into the rose-hued dress, zipping the back up all the way after some inventive shimmying. Then it's the hair. I stare at the blond mess, trying to conjure up some long lost memory of what Bri and Martina have done to it all those times before. I have to get it off my neck, or it will drive me insane, so I pull it back. The humidity is already making it a thick, wavy mass, so I let it look messy. It doesn't come out half bad, although I'm pretty sure Martina would roll her eyes at me and redo it herself.

I'm late, so I make the trek over to the grandstand by myself.

"There's the lady of the hour," Beck yells at me over the chorus of the grandstand. The race is a short one, so cheering begins early.

"Thanks for waiting up," I yell back at him, trotting down the stairs and slipping into the box, where he stands with my father and his parents—Laurence and Cynthia Delaney. I notice that Beck's other two siblings aren't around, which isn't too surprising. Matthew is out of college and embroiled in Wall Street. Olivia is sixteen and about as interested in the track as she is in getting her shoes dirty. She shows up for nothing less than the televised races, and the Dwyer and the Suburban are only stepping stone races to the big events. If Star wins the Dwyer, I'll expect to see her at Monmouth when we run in the televised Haskell.

Beck is the only one of his siblings who really took to the racing world. I can relate to that, given that I've been saddled with an older sister whom I now rarely see because she would rather not have the potent smell of horse manure clinging to her for the rest of the day.

Our horse doesn't win, but he gets up for third. He'll be one of our regulars at Saratoga, for sure. By the time the Dwyer rolls around several races later, I am sweating and rubbing the condensation of my newly purchased bottle of water against my forehead. In the saddling paddock, Beck wafts some of the stagnant air toward me with his battered program.

"You can say it, July," he says. "It's okay."

"I don't know what you mean," I say, and he scoffs, despite keeping up with the fanning. Some girl in his past must have trained him well, before he skedaddled right out of her company.

"I'll get you started," he says, still wafting away. "Thank . . ."

I narrow my eyes at him and he chooses to tap the end of the program against my nose. I snatch the booklet from him and he laughs.

Quark Star makes his one and only circuit around the spacious saddling paddock for the viewers, Dad's most regularly used jockey, Jorge Velazquez, on his back in Blackbridge's colors. Star makes the loop in an easy, professional walk, and then heads for the track. We file up into the stands.

Seven horses go to the post, and Star gives the gate crew one defiant hind kick, as if to say *don't bother pushing me* before walking right in. I watch him in the gate, can see Jorge working on the reins and the colt's head weaving left and right, despite the assistant starter's hold on the bridle. Then the gate opens and the horses are released onto the track.

Star is content to sit several lengths off the leader, but not so far back that he looks like he's dawdling. They race out of the chute and into the backstretch, Jorge sticking Star in a spot by the rail, racing in fifth. There's almost no pace in the race, which isn't so bad for us, but when fifth for Star usually means six or seven lengths back, this time he's actually only a few leaps away from overtaking four horses and making a break for it.

I can hear Dad's mumbling behind me, his way of saying that he doesn't like how this is going. We all stand silently, on the verge of yelling. When the horses gallop into the far turn, beginning the long stretch drive to the finish, none of us can take it anymore. The whole grandstand erupts from a low murmur to a rumbling roar, yells of encouragement carrying across the track. It reaches the jockeys and the horses as a discordant, disorienting noise. There's plenty of shouting going on in the race between the jocks you'd never hear over the grandstand and the thundering hooves.

Star is really running, slipping down the rail and making a scary move between horses so he can stretch out. I know he has it in the bag when he finally has room to go, because his long body unfolds, going faster when everyone else falls back.

Our colt wins by a good four lengths, and I'm breathless watching Star gallop out through the clubhouse turn. Another horse canters by Star, and the jockey slaps Jorge's shoulder in congratulations. Everyone knows what this means for us, but Beck's knuckles scrubbing against my scalp drives the knowledge home.

"Thinking about the Haskell, kiddo?"

I bat his hand away, but I can't help the smile.

Chapter Five

"This one," Martina tells me, pulling a dress out of my closet and throwing it on the bed. "And this one."

I don't pay attention, because I'm too busy trying to decide if I should bother taking anything to Saratoga that I can't reasonably ride in. The dresses Martina picks out won't see anything other than race days. I decide to go ahead and pack my favorite shirts, the ones that shouldn't under any circumstances be within touching distance of a horse, just in case.

"Do you remember that dark blue dress I have?" Martina asks me, not bothering to turn around. She's standing in the middle of my closet, her hands on her hips, surveying my dress situation. Her dark hair curls loosely all the way down her back, and she's still in her work clothes from the law firm where she's paid well to file papers and chat up people seeking disability. She looks a lot like Mom from my position on the other side of the room, and if I said that she would probably throw something at me, so I mutter a vague noise she can construe as yes.

"I think it would look good on you," she says to the closet.

"Thanks," I say, pulling my dusty, track-only duffel bag over and going through its contents. We're leaving for Saratoga tomorrow, but with the Haskell coming up and Quark

Star still preparing for it, there will be some interesting maneuvering to get most of the string situated at Blackbridge's training facility outside of Saratoga, and Star to Monmouth in Jersey.

Saratoga is the pinnacle of the New York circuit. I don't know why Mom ever wanted to leave it for Santa Anita. Before she left, Mom was in the top ten riders at Belmont. She was happy with what she had, but then, I don't know. She got restless, I guess. Maybe the New York circuit wore on her. Maybe the warm California sunshine and the freedom to bounce from track to track, horse to horse, was appealing.

The horse she permanently left New York for was called Separate Ways, after a Journey song. When I got older, I found a lot of hilarity in that. He came in fifth in the Derby that year. Since then, there have been a lot of horses like him for Mom.

Dad, of course, has had a lot of horses like him, too. He's never once asked Mom to come back to ride any of them.

"Are you sure you don't want to keep that dress here?" I ask Martina's back. "If you come up for any of the race days, you might want to bring it."

"I am house-sitting," Martina says with great resolution. "Remember?"

"Right," I nod, going back to the duffel. Everything is there, but I still go through it again, because I want to be sure.

Martina stands there for a second, like she doesn't know what to do, before she announces that she's going to get the dress and disappears. I have more dresses than I realistically need for this meet. Ten is way too many. It's Martina's doing, and I don't really contradict her. She would refuse to hear it.

When she comes back, I try again anyway. "Scott would like the races. You know it's right up his alley."

She frowns at me, putting the dress down on top of the others and opening up the garment bag. If there is one thing Martina is devoted to in life, it is packing clothing properly. "It's not Scott's thing," she corrects me. "And I'm not taking him."

"What if he wanted to come?"

"I still wouldn't go with him," she says easily. "It's not *my* thing, Juls. You know that, so stop asking."

"Fine."

"It's not that I don't want the horses to do well."

"I know."

"I don't want to be there."

"Okay."

"Okay?"

"I just said it was," I say, louder than necessary. I'm more than irritated that she never shows up, leaving me to be the one that has to deal with any potential insanity if and when Mom pops up in one of the programs, like she did at Aqueduct. Martina doesn't follow any of this, and she probably doesn't know the effort I put into making sure we'll never be surprised again, and she wouldn't be impressed or appreciative of my efforts. She'd ask me why I bother, because it's not as if I'm going to keep doing this racing thing as seriously as Dad.

At least, that's her opinion. I don't even know what mine is at the moment.

She pauses in her rapid packing to look at me from across the bed. "I'm sorry," she says, and I blink at her.

"I know you want me to come," she says, and shrugs. "But I'm not going to."

Well, at least we're being forthright now.

I could push her some more, but I don't. I don't have the willpower to keep fighting for some ray of hope that my sister will crack. Instead of continuing this exercise in futility, I zip up the duffel bag, push it over by my suitcase, and thank her for helping me pack.

Martina shrugs again, looking over her work with something akin to pride. "Someone has to do this," she says. "If I left it all up to you there wouldn't be a day during Saratoga that you had something to wear that was wrinkle-free."

"My clothes and sense of fashion commend you, Martina."

She does catch the sarcasm. "You know, for someone so persnickety about *everything*, you're remarkably slovenly."

And this is where I'm ending this conversation.

I pick up my keys and grab my bag. "I'm going to Woodfield."

"The old barn?" Martina asks, like it's never occurred to her to go to the barn. She used to be all about it once upon a time. "Don't you ever go anywhere normal?"

"Apparently not," I say, pulling my newest pair of breeches out of my drawer of riding clothes, leaving the room and Martina behind me.

～

My car crunches onto gravel and lurches into a pothole as soon as I turn into the drive of Woodfield Equestrian Center, my home away from the racing circuit. I mutter a curse at the riddled gravel lot and manage to avoid the other massive pits and ridges on my way to the barn, an imposing structure that looks like it's about to fall down.

I'm sure the Hempstead residents around this tiny piece of property would like nothing more than for the barn to magically disappear, if the banner that's draped over the barn door declaring "Save Woodfield!" is any indication. The whole place is nothing more than the barn, the giant outdoor arena, and the most overgrown one-acre paddock I've ever seen. Still, there are thirty horses situated in that barn, and this is where, one day, Diver could spend his time rehabbing from the track if I can somehow buy him.

Woodfield is where I learned to ride. I come back when there's time, of which lately there's been none.

"Juls!" Lisa, my old riding instructor, yells at me as soon as I get out of the car. She's lunging a muscular bay in the arena, her attention solely on the horse, and I wonder how she even noticed my arrival. "Go tack up Gideon. We moved him to second aisle, on the left. Everything else is the same."

I slam the door. "Good to see you too, Leese."

She nods her head up in acknowledgement, her brown ponytail bobbing.

The barn is cool inside, the piercing summer sun and heat hardly penetrating the three long aisles. It smells strongly of horses and manure, dust floating everywhere, but it's far cleaner than Barn 27, and that's something I appreciate. Gideon is vacuuming down his hay, shoving half of it out onto the cement aisle in his enthusiasm. When he sees me coming he barely spares me a glance, probably because I don't have anything enticing to convince him that hay isn't all life's cracked up to be.

I give Gideon a once over with a brush and tack him up in his stall, get his galloping boots in place, snatch up one of the long dressage whips, and take him out into the shocking afternoon light. He blinks at the sudden transformation, and thinks about yelling out to the horse Lisa has on the lunge line before making a grunt in the back of his throat, as if to say, *eh, forget it.*

He decides instead to snort in my face.

"Thanks for that," I tell him, while he perks up and swings his hips around all the way to the gate.

Gideon has several years on me and he spent most of my formative years saving my ass while I learned how to ride. He's the barn's star schoolmaster, and riding him is like a slice of nostalgia. It's always peaceful, right before he comes to a dead halt from a canter because dust clouds are terrifying and mysterious. I've flipped over his shoulder more times than I'd like to admit. My first broken bone? Totally received while falling from Gideon.

Lisa's still working with the bay, which has gone into some acrobatic leaps on the lunge that I'm sure Gideon doesn't have in him anymore, so I wait by the gate and spectate. Lisa watches the bay like an intense hawk focuses on prey, and the horse is wild-eyed as it flings its mane. I watch the endless circling, Lisa's commands and the thudding sounds of hooves on soft dirt lulling me into a trance. Gideon takes that moment to nip me on the arm and I jump. He jumps in response. I shake my head at him and rub at the abused skin that's already turning an angry pink. There will be the tiniest of bruises on my arm tomorrow, courtesy of this crazy gelding.

The bay calms down and Lisa brings it to a halt. "Come on in, Juls," she says to me, breathing heavily after the effort with the bay. I lead Gideon inside the arena, eying the new recruit.

"Who's he?" I ask, pulling down the stirrups to Gideon's saddle and mounting up.

"She," Lisa says, scrubbing her dirty fingers over the mare's forehead. The mare gives Gideon what can only be described as a glare, so I keep him on the other half of the arena, making Lisa talk across the distance. "She's my new show horse in training. I thought she'd be a new school horse, but turns out she hates it."

"Not everyone can be as easygoing as Gideon," I say, walking the gelding on a loose rein and using a nudge here and there to guide him around in a circle. "I like the look of her, though."

"There's potential," Lisa says, ever sparing with her praise. She leads the mare out of the arena and yells over her shoulder, "Keep walking him on the buckle. I'll be back in a second and we'll see how rusty you are."

I wince, wondering what she's going to put me through. I haven't been around in a while, true. It used to be that I'd be here all the time after school, mucking out stalls and doing stupid things like galloping Gideon around bareback in the lonely pasture with other working students my age. I've done a lot of dressage shows in this arena, and in the larger farms further out on Long Island, back when I had the time and I wasn't single-mindedly pursuing a slip of memory in the form of my mother.

I gather up Gideon's reins and push him into a faster walk. We accomplish a bunch of walk-trot transitions on one side of the arena, Gideon warming up and me trying not to think about anything. The gelding snorts and keeps trying to stick his left side against my leg as we turn, throwing a kink into the works. A nudge doesn't get the point across, so I flick the whip behind my boot. He shifts his barrel to the right, precisely where I want it, and we flow into the circle.

That's when Lisa shows up and reprimands me for starting the lesson early.

"In my defense," I say, bringing Gideon to a halt in the center of the arena as she walks up and stops in front of us, hands on her hips, "I didn't know I was signing on for a lesson."

"Whatever," Lisa says, pushing my boot with the side of her hand. Gideon steps away from the pressure obediently. "You're going to Saratoga tomorrow, right? You've made squeezing in an extra lesson a summer tradition, so why stop now that you're barely around?"

I make a face. A guilty, pathetic face.

"Figure eights," Lisa says. "Sitting trot. I will settle for no less than perfection."

An hour later, Gideon and I are soaked in sweat. We've done every riding exercise I can think of off the top of my head, and since Lisa has chosen this day to reintroduce me to counter-canter I feel like my brain is about to explode. Gideon has taken it into his head to come to a dead halt every time I do it wrong, and the fifth time we come out of the turn and loop away from the wall on the correct lead, I think to myself that *this is it*. If we don't get it right this time around, Gideon will probably try to kill me.

By some miracle, it all clicks. Gideon loops away from the wall, drifts back in like the professional he is, and we flow through the turn. There's two strides of me letting out a celebratory whoop to release all that repressed frustration, and Gideon does what I should have expected and comes to such a bone-shuddering stop that I find myself up on his neck and clinging to his coarse mane.

"Hey, Juls, save the partying for afterward," Lisa advises from her spot in the middle of the arena. I push myself off of Gideon's neck and wiggle back into the saddle, sliding back onto the leather with a tremulous sigh. Gideon, the little angel, stands still the entire time.

"I'll try to remember that," I say, leaving my feet out of the stirrups and dangling. I give Gideon two hearty pats on the shoulder and dismount, which mostly equates to falling down because my legs hit the ground and fold. I roll onto my back and can't help laughing, while Gideon shuffles his nose across my stomach and nudges the pockets of my breeches, still finding nothing to eat.

"Okay, crazy girl," Lisa sighs, her dusty boots coming into vision by my head. She offers me her hand, and I take it, letting her pull me up to my feet. "I know dressage can't kick your ass."

"Point taken," I say, undoing my helmet and tugging it off. I swipe at the dirt that's coating my butt and thighs. "This is still exhausting."

Lisa loosens Gideon's girth and says, "You need to come by more often. Riding those racers every morning isn't cutting it."

I laugh again, because that's not at all the case and Lisa knows it. Riding racers every morning is death defying. "One of these days," I say. "When I get Diver from Delaney, he'll need a good place to wind down after racing. I'll board him here, and then you'll never get rid of me."

"You still haven't bought that horse yet?" Lisa asks, well-versed in my obsession with eventually owning Diver. "Hasn't that been your primary goal for the past I don't know how long?"

"Since Mom left," I shrug, "but I'm not counting years or anything."

"With your lack of execution in the horse purchasing department, I wouldn't be either," she says, pulling Gideon's reins over his head while I run up the stirrups. My skin goes red, like it commonly does when I'm faced with facts I don't much like.

"Well," I sigh, "one of these days he has to start sucking on the track, right?"

"One of these days," Lisa agrees, but then she shrugs. "I'll have a stall for him should that day ever occur."

We walk Gideon back up to the barn, the barn I'll see all the time the moment Diver sets foot inside. It will be home away from home again, and I hope that will be soon.

Chapter Six

Blackbridge Farm is a few miles south of Saratoga Springs, all black fences and rolling green hills. One side is dedicated to breeding, housing priceless mares and foals still unsteady on their feet. The other side of the farm is all racing, stabling the fleet next to a training track that loops between the forest and the main house. Blackbridge is where I've spent most of my summers since I was twelve. In a lot of ways, it's the summer cottage my family never had.

It's here that we'll keep all the horses instead of stabling them in rented stalls at the racecourse. Our caravan arrives at Blackbridge a couple of days before the meet officially begins, because we've got horses to acclimate before they race on opening day. It's a lot of work to load and unload over half a racing stable in one day, even when we have plenty of help and a game plan.

Blackbridge has been ready for us days beforehand, and we've got a long list of directions for each horse, but there's almost always confusion, and horses are never predictable. To make matters worse, it's pouring rain. When Lighter, our eternal screw up, refuses to get off the trailer for a good twenty minutes, and then suddenly barrels off of it and smacks Gus's head against the opening for the ramp, I think for a minute we'll have an ambulance show up for the first time in our six years of moving horses to Blackbridge.

"I'm okay, Juls," Gus insists when I inspect the gash on the side of his temple, but I shake my head because it is really not okay.

"Stitches," I say with certainty, and he winces. I do too, because there's a lot of blood seeping into his shirt, and I'm making him hold a towel to the side of his head.

That's how I spend three hours in the emergency room with Gus, who is afraid of doctors, needles, and anything vaguely hospital related. I don't know how he manages his own line of work, because horse injuries can be bloody.

"That horse," he mutters while his head is stitched back up. I nod and pat his arm, because between the two of us, nothing more really needs to be said.

Afterward the rain lets up and Gus treats me to take out in exchange for driving him to the emergency room. We decide to bring enough food back to Blackbridge to feed an army, because it's almost time for our hard working team to eat something and I know I'm starved. I can't contain myself and crack into a container of French fries on our way back home.

I pull into a spot closest to the main training barn, and pop the trunk.

"What did you guys get up to?" Izzie says, coming out of the barn when she sees us, her eyes lighting up when I pull the white bags out of the trunk. "Is that what I think it is?"

"It is," I say, motioning her over to help. She jumps over, smacking Gus on the shoulder and telling him he should change his shirt before he handles any of the food, because head injuries around here aren't all that big of a deal if they can be fixed in a couple of hours. He rolls his eyes at her and strips his shirt off, much to her glee. His tattoos run over his shoulders and pour down the sides of his torso, all Mexican pride and Day of the Dead skulls.

"Don't be too mature," I tell them, carrying an armload of juicy junk food into the stable.

"I wouldn't dream of it, Juls." Izzie calls behind me, helping Gus with the rest of the food and liter bottles of soda.

Our arrival means the beginning of break time for everyone in the vicinity. Even Dad drops what he's doing and grabs something to eat. There isn't anywhere to sit, so we mostly laze around in the aisle or lean against the walls. I opt to sit outside of Maggie's stall, feeding her the slices of carrot I brought with me from home while I eat my hamburger. Kali drapes her neck over the door of her neighboring stall, smacking her lips at my bag of carrots until I count out a few for her.

"How's Gus?" Dad asks, easing himself down next to me and sipping at his soda.

"Okay," I say, peering down the aisle where Gus and Izzie are bickering over the last of the fries. "He didn't faint in the ER, so I guess it went well enough."

Dad nods his head, like this is the best we can expect. "When will the stitches have to come out?"

I shrug. "Week or so."

"You'll need to remind him about that," he says. "Because he won't want to remember."

"He'll regret it if he doesn't want to remember."

"Juls."

"I'll make sure he goes back," I say, because looking after the employees became my unofficial role the instant it became obvious that almost no one around here could resist me when I was a kid. I keep waiting for that to slip, because I'm nearly eighteen now, no longer exactly cute as a button, but Dad has low turnover, and people like Gus have been with us for a long time. Long enough to remember me when I was little. Dad knows how to use that to his advantage, and to Gus's, it seems.

"Why don't you head up to the apartment after this," he says, finishing up his soda and standing up. "I think we have everything down here."

This is his way of telling me that the apartment needs to be fixed up. There are plenty of places to stay at Blackbridge during the summer; employee apartments are on the premises and there are several miniature mansions dotting the property for trainers and farm managers. But our apartment has always been the one that's above the main training barn, as close to the horses as humanly possible.

The key in the lock is sticky, but it opens the door. Dust drifts in the air. I walk around the perimeter of the apartment, opening windows. Then I go over to the sliding door and yank at it until it slides open all the way, which is good because going out on the balcony is one of the things I love about this place. It's nice to stand there in the morning and watch the works on the training oval, which takes up the whole field nearby.

I check the kitchen, noticing nothing but a box of baking soda in the refrigerator and a collection of spices that have probably solidified in their jars. Shopping has to happen immediately if I'm going to eat something other than old cumin for breakfast. I do a cursory once over of the place until it's somewhat livable.

I grab my keys and head back out to my car, yelling at Dad that I'll be back in an hour or two. On my way to the car, I pass by Beck, who's walking back from one of the pad-docks with a leather lead swinging from his fingers. He's got on his normal apparel: faded jeans and T-shirt, only this time the material across his chest has been smeared by the greenish hue of horse saliva.

"Whoa, hold up," he says, breaking into a jog and tossing the lead onto a pile of their kindred inside the stable door. He's smiling that stupid, goofy smile. Like it's supposed to affect me or something.

"What?" I ask him, and he comes to a stop in front of me, gravel skidding under his shoes.

"Where you goin'?"

"To the store." I open the car door and pause, turning toward him. "What are you doing here?"

"What do you mean by that?" He's still all smiles. "It's summer. It's Saratoga."

I had assumed Beck would keep his fairly predictable schedule of rarely showing up, but I suppose I'm wrong. Now he's making himself handy around the stable, which is odd for many reasons, but concerning because this means he'll more than happily stick around to enforce a stupid bet.

He's like that. It's irritating.

"That doesn't tell me anything," I say, leaning into the open door. He moseys over to my car, resting one hand against the roof and looking at me in that way that screams he doesn't need a reason. He goes where he wants, does what he wants, and cavalierly skips through life like he's never graduated past the simple joys of getting a free lollipop at the bank.

"I'm tired of the city," is his vague answer. "And I have a bet to see through."

"Right," I scoff, although with him you never really know. "How about you give me a real reason and I'll let you come with me to Price Chopper."

"That's not really what I call an incentive."

"For your information," I tell him, all haughty, which I know he likes because he can't seem to convince himself to keep out of my reach. He knows I can and will smack him in the arm, because when he's around on a consistent basis I average about two well-placed punches per week. "You'll miss out on the most fantastic shopping experience ever."

"Oh, July," he says, leaning against my car. "You are really not prepared to throw those sort of statements around."

"Shut up," I tell him. "And get off my car."

He lifts his hands and himself, acting innocent. I get in the car, turn on the engine, and begin to back up. Outside my window, Beck is there. He slaps the door panel of the car like he would with a horse he's pleased with, and walks back to the barn.

~

Usually there's some welcome dinner that we're always subjected to after the first full day we spend at Blackbridge. Over the years it's become a bit of a ceremonial tradition, morphing from quiet get-together to farm party, but this year there's no sign that this annual bash ever existed. The day slips by, slowly fades to night, and I watch the twilight wink out in the sky with my booted feet resting against the balcony railing of the loft apartment.

Dad's light snoring from the sofa means he's already out for the night, too exhausted to remove himself to his bed. I am right there with him, but it's finally nice outside—cool after the rain—and I want to enjoy it while I can. By tomorrow morning it will be too muggy to breathe comfortably.

I pull out my cell phone and find Martina's number in my recent contacts, then hope she'll pick up. It's not exactly wise of me to call her, because she knows that I don't trust her with the house, and I also know that this enrages her.

I can't help it, though. It's an impulse. I suppose Martina's right when she tells me I'm a control freak. It's not really that bad, though. I'm a control freak when it comes to not having to pick up over a month's worth of mess when I get home. If Martina allowed herself to realize how disgusting she can be, we'd all be better off and I'd get in less screaming matches with her about clean sinks and the utilization of cutting boards and the art of washing cookie sheets. It is an art, damn it. It is.

"I swear to god, July," Martina says when she picks up the phone, bypassing any greeting. "I haven't burned down the house."

"Maybe I wanted to call to tell you we're all fine and nothing bad happened on the way to Blackbridge," I say, trying not to sound infinitely smug. She sees right through it.

"I don't think so," Martina says. "You're worried."

"Perhaps," I say slowly. "Or perhaps Dad's asleep and I'm bored. What are you doing?"

"Nothing that I want to talk about," Martina says, her words clipped and final. "I've got to go. Call you later?"

"I guess . . ."

But she's already skipping to the goodbye and the phone winds up dead by my ear. That's really rather typical.

I send a random text to Bri, but it goes unanswered.

I stare out at the main residence, watch the few bright windows, and wonder for a moment what is so off about this year. It can't be the lack of a party, the fact that Gus got his head smashed into a trailer, the reemergence of Beck. They're such small things. A figure drifts by one of the lit windows, Beck's outline blurry and nondescript from where I am on the balcony, so far away. It pauses, and I watch it steadily, before the light extinguishes.

Inside, Dad is still snoring away, a blatant reminder that the day will come soon enough.

Chapter Seven

I t's entirely too early when I hear the words, "So where's my mare?"

I've just walked down the stairs from the loft, a travel mug of steaming hot coffee warming the palm of my hand, and the morning is still dark, cool, and blissfully quiet. It's chilly to be standing here in jeans and a tank top, and it's surreal to have Beck standing in front of me at this hour, in saddle-worn jeans and a black T-shirt that says *I Support Single Moms* printed across his chest like a chauvinistic banner. His hair sticks up all over the place, proof that he hasn't bothered with a shower. He's got about as much eagerness as a hyperactive puppy that desperately wants to dig for no reason.

"You mean Maggie?" I ask, stumbling to a stop and giving him a wary once over to make sure he hasn't totally lost his mind. He looks like any other exercise rider I've ever seen, and I'm happy to note that his boots are his old broken in pair. I'm stunned that he still has them.

"That's the one," he says, rubbing his hands together like he's really genuinely got to do this and absolutely relishes the very idea. I take a sip of my coffee, wondering how he is this bright eyed and bushy tailed. He must be on his third cup of coffee by now, if the way he's bouncing on his toes is any indication.

"Okay, Mr. Cheerful," I tell him, "what do you have planned with my mare?"

"You tell me," he says. "This was your plan."

I pause, because I really hadn't anticipated following the bet up with action. It wasn't like I was serious about offering up Maggie, was I? Didn't I say something about Diver? Where was my brain when I said those things? Beck wasn't even supposed to be here.

"If I remember correctly, you were to show up after Lighter fabulously loses his first race," I say. "We just got here. Opening day hasn't even started yet. Seriously, why are you here?"

He bounces again on the balls of his feet. "A smart man once said that fortune favors the prepared mind."

Oh, boy.

"Think you can handle her?"

He gives me a look.

I bite my lip, because everything I said is perfectly true. He can handle Maggie, and Diver, and probably Lighter if he wanted to. It's just that now, being presented with the reality of what I proffered a month ago, this doesn't seem like the best plan. Not only am I giving him Maggie, but he's going to be *here*. All the time.

Then Dad has to arrive and I remember with relief that he can veto all of it.

"Beck."

Fabulous. This will be easily fixed. I turn around to see my father, who's trotting down the steps sans coffee, because he's gotten in a full eight hours of sleep and is never swayed to break his rule that one must be dead to the world by seven o'clock at night. What does a man like him need with coffee?

"Hey, Rob." Beck smiles winningly at Dad, and then nods over to me. "July is offering Maggie to me this morning. Sweet of her, huh?"

Dad gives me a curious look and shrugs. "Whatever she likes. You're planning on riding with us this summer?"

Beck pauses for the most minute of seconds, and I can already tell he was expecting a reaction that was slightly less blasé. Dad is treating this as if Beck wanting to ride in the mornings was perfectly expected. Beck narrows his eyes at me, and I concentrate on my travel mug, taking another sip while I pretend to not pay much attention.

"So far, that is the very rough plan."

"Good, that will free up July. I've got a fleet of youngsters and I need another rider." Dad smiles, looking between us like he can't decide whether or not to be confused or amused. He's managing an intriguing combination of both, mainly all of these looks aimed right at me, before he claps one hand over Beck's shoulder, shaking him like he's testing his balance, and then strolls off down the aisle.

Beck looks like he's swallowing down a thousand questions, like he hadn't expected that simplistic of a response. My immediate dismay at the situation is suddenly tempered by my enjoyment at the shock on his face. Maybe this won't be so bad after all, especially when Lighter finishes up the track and I am victorious. Sure, I'll give Beck points for showing up and acting eager, but he had to be suspecting Dad would turn him right around and send him back home.

Own it, July, I think.

I scoot past him, peeking behind me as I head for the tack room. He's scrubbing a hand through his hair, still slack-jawed from being played by someone far superior to him. I smile, very superiorly. Then I call, "Hey, Beck, let me show you where Maggie's tack is."

He turns, slowly. I raise my eyebrows, waving at him from the tack room door. He takes his time walking up to me, this glint of cheerful malice that should probably concern me, but I'm too busy smiling, totally self-satisfied for the moment.

"There will be a time and a place, July," he tells me, lowering his head so only I can hear him. I don't doubt there's going to be some retribution this summer. I wonder if we're too old for pranks involving dyed shampoo?

"I'm sure," I reply, and then point at Maggie's bulky Western saddle. He picks it up in one hand and snags the bridle I hand him, then stalks off without a word.

∿

We're changing it up with Kali, who has made it to Saratoga with us not because of her blinding talent but because there's always another claiming race to enter her in. The smallest hope is that someone will pick her up out of a claimer and turn her into something she's actually good at. This can be a likely fate, but it's all up to chance. I don't so much like chance. So I sit on Kali and let her take her time this morning, although this is hard because Beck is out there, transformed from pouting about having to actually do the work he's come here for to actually embracing it full on.

He canters toward the first turn with Galaxy Collision on the end of his line, sitting the gait like he's been doing it for years and could never forget. He's impressively picked the whole thing up again, giving cues to Maggie that I can barely see. She does a lead change to the left as they enter the turn, like a racer. I can't help watching, wondering if Beck remembers how to do that when he's riding a breezing racehorse. Probably so, if today is any indication.

With a flick of his wrist, Beck lets go of Galaxy. The filly rockets off, leaving them in her dust.

I sit on Kali, letting her soak up the scenery a bit more, because she's the last of my day and we're doing nothing more than one long, loose gallop. The filly pricks her ears at Maggie, who digs in her haunches and transitions into a walk without stumbling over her feet. Beck gives the mare a pat on her splotchy neck.

"And you were concerned about this?" I ask him, watching him slide Maggie to a halt in front of me.

"We all can't be as cool and confident as you are, Juls." Then he waves a hand at Kali. "You planning on doing anything with her, or did I take you down here for a soak in the sun?"

"Kali likes to take her time."

"Ah, so this is the morning glory," Beck says, looking the filly over curiously. It surprises me that he remembers her now. It further surprises me that he knows her as a morning glory. Leave it to Beck to be so blunt.

I gather Kali's reins and move her past Beck and Maggie, who stay put by the outside rail. Kali goes through her paces, shifting into a gallop without any trouble and going the full length of the training oval and then some before we ease back. Not too much, or too little. In the back of my head, I wonder what claimer she'll be in next. What day will it be? How long do we have?

I stop myself right there. There's no point to driving myself crazy about it. Kali is a claimer, and I'll accept that because I have to. I swallow down the lump in my throat and slip slide in the smooth leather of the saddle. Dad will do right by her, changing it up, switching tactics, but it's a racing barn first. I shouldn't dwell over this filly's future, especially when it couldn't be a less convenient time.

Kali walks purposefully down the outside rail, back the way we came, alert and happy. I take my feet out of the stirrups and move with her body.

"Not too bad," Beck says when we reach him. "Must be something to that morning glory term after all."

Something in me finally snaps. He reaches out to take the filly's bridle. "Don't," I say, and he pauses, his hand falling back to rest on his leg as we walk the horses back to the gap. "We can go on our own."

Beck doesn't say a word, and my fingers twitch rhythmically on the reins. Kali lowers her head, plays with the bit, and I let her lengthen her stride, walking ahead of Beck and Maggie back to the barn.

"So what was that about?" Beck asks when I've hopped off of Kali and have handed her over to a very doting Izzie. The filly and groom disappear back outside, where Izzie will make no secret that the filly is her favorite. Kali probably gets more peppermints and personal attention than most of the best racehorses in the barn, all thanks to Izzie's refusal to let things like victories and talent get in the way of pure affection.

Kali is a sweet filly. She deserves it.

"Nothing," I say, lost in thought as I come out of the tack room.

"Hey, July," he says, lifting his right leg over Maggie's neck and landing with a muted thunk on the cement ground. "What was that?"

"I didn't need you to help take her back," I say without much conviction or sincerity. It's a bland statement, one that Beck doesn't look like he believes.

He pulls Maggie's reins over her head, undoes the cinch and hauls the Western saddle off to expose the wide swatch of sweat covering my mare's back. I pull off my crash helmet and bandana, glad I've braided my hair back away from my face. It's a hot day, and the more I take off, away from my skin, the better. I pull the protective vest off and dump it in Dad's office with the helmet and bandana, walking up to Maggie and swapping her bridle with her halter, clipping on a lead and handing the bridle off to Beck when he comes back from dealing with the saddle.

"She needs to get hosed down," I say curtly, leading Maggie past him. He follows aimlessly, watching me take her around Kali and Izzie, to the second hose stationed along the side of the barn. He doesn't offer to help while I turn on the hose, soaking Maggie down from hooves to head, lingering on her sweaty places, and then leading her away soaking wet.

I lead her right up to Beck and say, "Hold her."

He takes the lead without a word, and I walk over to Izzie to borrow her scraper, trudging back, my jeans and boots damp and dirty now, to press the water out of Maggie's coat.

"Are you going to be this helpful every day?" I ask Beck when I come back from leaving the scraper with Izzie, snagging the lead from his hands.

"Hey, I'm just riding them," is what he dares say to me.

I shake my head and walk Maggie off to one of the pastures, letting her loose for some grazing time. When I close the gate behind me, coiling the lead in my hands, I turn and there he is again, appearing confused.

"What did I say?" he asks, and I don't know what it is that has me up in arms. Or, more accurately, I don't know what it was that had me so irritated before he made that stupid remark about "just riding them."

"If you're going to ride Maggie, you're taking care of her, too," I tell him, ignoring for a moment that this is not what pissed me off before. It's convenient that he said something so easy to latch onto, because even if he was about to do all the things I just did, he had to open his big mouth and indicate that he wasn't even thinking about it.

"That's not what you're angry about," he says, and *ugh*. Thanks a lot for being so astute, Beck.

"Yes, it is," I say, everything in me singing avoid, avoid, avoid. "She may be my horse, which I suppose to you means there's some leeway here, but when you're riding her, treat her as you would your own damn horse."

"Okay," he says slowly, "I guess I'll go along with this, because you've obviously gone crazy."

He lets out an exasperated curse right before he brightens, like he's stumbled across the greatest find in the history of trying to figure out what makes me tick. I scowl at him.

"This isn't about Maggie, it's about what I said about Kali. Aw, July. Is that your heart showing?"

"What?"

Beck looks like he just discovered the Holy Grail. Like he holds the key to understanding my moods, which, granted,

I'd like to have for myself. "I thought you wanted Diver when he was finished racing, not Kali."

"This is so not a normal conversation, and yes I do want Diver."

"But you don't want Kali claimed."

"I don't like seeing any horse claimed," I go on. "It's not exactly a fun time to see a horse you've worked with taken away to go be a success or an utter failure somewhere else, especially when she's so good in the mornings. It's a training issue, and it's frustrating. That's all."

He smiles, throwing an arm around my shoulders and bringing me in for this ridiculous, brotherly hug that pisses me off more. "You are such a girl, July."

I sigh. "Get off of me."

"And miss this wonderful bonding moment?"

I push him off and head for the barn. He follows behind me, not saying anything. Only the crunch of gravel indicates that he's back there at all, probably with a satisfied smirk on his face. When I walk back into the barn, Pilar and Izzie are there, car keys dangling from Pilar's hand.

"Where are you guys going?"

"Lunch," Izzie says. "I'm starved. Want to come with?"

"Absolutely," I say.

"What, and I'm not invited?" Beck asks, and I turn around.

"No," I say. "As penance for not helping me with Maggie, you are not invited."

He walks off, muttering something under his breath that I am sure would have been an open invitation for me to hit him in the arm. He really deserves it, and even my father's repeated insistence that I not beat up the owner's son doesn't really sway my opinion.

"So where are we going?" I ask.

"Bailey's," Pilar says. "Go get changed."

I don't have to be told twice.

∽

Saratoga sits in the heavy, bright heat around us. Flowers bloom out of their containers and the splashy, colorful Victorians are rubbed raw by the sun. The spa town booms in the summer, and everyone keeps an eye on the goings-on at the racecourse.

Izzie gets a table outside, because like a true outdoors girl she doesn't even stop to think that the indoors has air conditioning. It's still sweltering out, but there's a light enough breeze and my hair is still back in its braid, so I don't disagree with this decision. The huge glass of diet soda that is placed before me minutes later helps even more.

"Maybe I can get you to take Gus back to the hospital to get his stitches out," I tell her, playing with my straw while we're waiting for the food to get here. Izzie laughs like I've lost my mind, and certainly she isn't going to be the one to clean up the pieces of my compromised sanity.

"He can take himself," she huffs, which makes me smile because they've been on and off for at least two years.

"You know he won't go by himself."

"And that's his stupid fault," Izzie sniffs. They must be off again, no matter how they keep gazing after each other. They run hot and cold faster than tap water, I swear. "I don't have the time," Izzie insists, picking at the dirt under her newly bright blue nails. "In fact, I'm pretty sure the only person who has time around here is Beck, and I don't see that happening."

"He can surprise you," I say.

"Speaking of," Pilar says, waving some of the breeze her way with a flimsy paper napkin, "why was he riding Maggie this morning?"

I tell Pilar all about it, and she shakes her head.

"That's definitely not normal," she says, then leans forward and lowers her voice to a conspiratorial whisper. "And there's no one else at the house yet. Have you noticed that?"

I have noticed that.

"Why would Beck be the only one here?" I ask, dropping my voice as well.

Izzie and Pilar glance at each other, an unspoken understanding passing between them, and then back at me. Izzie shrugs, but Pilar opens and closes her mouth, like she's thought better of whatever she was going to say.

"Come on," I say, urging Pilar, who shifts uncomfortably, wadding up the paper cover for her straw. "I'll keep pestering you until you say something. What is it?"

Pilar knows me too well. "It's only rumors, and they're pretty worthless."

"I still want to know."

Pilar pauses again, and Izzie kicks at her legs. She misses Pilar completely and kicks the table, sending silverware rattling. Pilar throws her wadded straw wrapper at her.

"The word is that Delaney is still in Manhattan," Pilar says. "That he might not come up to Saratoga at all this year."

Delaney always comes to Saratoga. He's been coming to Saratoga since he was an infant, fifty some years ago. If it was true and he was staying in Manhattan this summer, there would have to be significant reason, so significant that the thought makes me pause.

"What would keep him in Manhattan?"

It's Pilar's turn to shrug. "It's just rumors."

But I have a feeling, almost immediately, that it's not.

Chapter Eight

Bronzy is a classically plain bay. She's gangly, because she'll be a big mare when she's older and is already big now. The only thing dainty about her is the tiny white star on her forehead, because the rest is impressively large.

"We want to go easy with her," Dad tells Jorge. "She'll want to go straight to the lead, so let her pull you out there."

We're in the saddling paddock at Saratoga, and it's opening day. Bronzy will run in her first race, a maiden for two-year-old fillies, those who are all first timers or have never won. The track is crawling with people. Families picnic in the shade of the trees, sprawled out in lawn chairs like they're at a particularly formal day at the beach. Gamblers rove between the saddling paddock, the bettor's windows, and the grandstand, going through a constant loop. The smell of cigar smoke drifts through the air, and it makes me want to heave.

I twist around when the smell gets stronger, wishing for a moment that whoever it is that has the damnable object would stub it out or go somewhere else. This isn't possible when I see that it's perched in Beck's fingers.

He saunters up to me, entourage at his back, and I almost have to blink and keep my mouth from dropping open. He's wearing this three-piece suit that makes him look like he stepped out of some black and white movie, and my mouth goes instantly dry. All I can think is that it's not fair. It's not fair that I am having this reaction to this boy in that suit and he looks at me like I could very well be wearing my normal jeans and T-shirt when I'm wearing this dress that flutters around my knees.

I look good, damn it. It would be nice to get a reaction for once.

"What are you doing?" I ask, grinding my teeth together to keep my mouth closed as I lean away from him.

"Here to see the horse," he says, putting the cigar between his lips. He's not really inhaling it, but it reeks and I can't begin to understand what he thinks the positives about this are. So I pluck it from his mouth and hold it between us.

"You can't take this into the grandstand."

"So I'll get rid of it."

"Now?"

"Are you always this much of a killjoy, or has it been a more recent development?"

"It smells horrible," I say, holding the cigar back out to him.

"It's opening day," he says, taking the stinky thing from me and putting it back in his mouth. He grins around the damp end of the cigar and saunters off. "Live a little."

I watch him as he shifts into the crowd, his hands in his pockets and pale smoke drifting over his head. I wrinkle my nose, deciding to not focus on the stretch of space between his shoulder blades in that ridiculous suit and more on the smell. That's probably a much safer choice for me.

So now I'm going to smell like cigar smoke, which has got to be the first downward development of the day. Right after the revelation that Beck in a suit is suddenly sexy instead of vaguely irritating. Everything had been going swimmingly so far. The horses shipped the few miles to the racetrack without even the slightest hitch, they all settled into their temporary stalls for the day, and even more amazing, we won the opening race. All was going great until Beck showed up with his cigar and an entourage.

I give the two guys and three girls a quick once over, at least somewhat satisfied that none of them are smoking. When one of the tall, willowy girls with super shiny blond hair turns to look at me, smiling as Beck says something and takes the cigar out of his mouth, I let my gaze slide by. I don't recognize any of them, because over the years I've gotten to know absolutely none of Beck's high school and society friends. They're the upper crust type, and while I appreciate that slice of demographics, it doesn't mean I'm all too comfortable with them.

Here is where Bri would be rolling her eyes. I wish I had pockets in this dress, or at least had thought to bring a purse to keep my cell phone. I need to text her about visiting for the Travers Stakes, because Bri always comes up to Saratoga for at least one weekend, whichever one has the best of our horses running in the biggest race. This year, I'm betting it will be Star.

I am all too happy when Dad shoves Bronzy's lead rope in my hands. "Take her around, Juls."

I blink at him, but shrug and lead Bronzy out of the open-air stall. She follows me patiently, letting me guide her down the walkway. Gus hangs back behind me. Sometimes, Dad likes to have me take the horses around the paddock, because a girl in a pretty dress is better to look at than Gus, or so the theory goes. I'm sure most of the women in the crowd would prefer Gus and his tattoos.

"How are the stitches?" I ask him, and Gus lifts a hand up to his temple, drawing a fingertip over the black knots that dot up the wound.

"They itch," he says, and I smile.

"When do they have to come out again?"

He frowns at me.

"Don't be like that. Izzie will drag you back there if you're not careful."

"I can take myself." He sighs, like he's long suffering. Between Izzie and Lighter, he probably is, but his life isn't much more different than anyone else's in the barn.

"Promise?"

"Sure, I promise. You're a slave driver, July." He narrows his eyes at me, but it's all for show. Because then he smiles, all even white teeth. Gus puts a hand between my shoulder blades and pushes, and I skip forward to evade another playful shove. The filly lifts her head and snorts, taking a few trotting steps with me.

We pass by Beck and his friends, and I can't help letting myself take a few quick glances in their direction. I notice that Beck has gotten rid of the cigar. I walk by, hiding my smile against Bronzy's mane.

~~

Bronzy doesn't win. In fact, she's got a lot of improvement to do, but her failure to finish well doesn't put a damper on anyone's enthusiasm over opening day. Beck gives me a wink when he walks by with his friends, his skinny blond girl doing an admirable job as arm candy. Thankfully Beck doesn't notice the hot blush rising up my skin, too busy saying something to the girl as she pushes ironed locks of nearly white hair behind her ear. Sparkling stones dangle from her earlobes, and whatever she's looking at is hidden behind oversized sunglasses.

I turn quickly to Bronzy and let Beck's flighty attention slip out of my mind. When Bronzy is cooled off and bathed, we bypass her temporary stall and load her right into the van. I help with the rest of the horses, leading them up the metal ramp and into the dark confines within, securing them and hopping back down to the gravel.

This will be a daily event in my life for the rest of the summer, so it's best to work quickly and get out. We all want to get home, which is still unusually quiet when we arrive.

The rumors so far are true. Delaney hasn't shown up yet, and he always shows up for opening day. Instead it's Beck and whomever he brought with him, which gives all of this a vibe I dislike. It feels empty, wrong and disturbing, like we're all uninvited houseguests, playing with the owner's things while they're not at home.

Maybe I'm overreacting. If Beck looks like there's nothing to be bothered by, maybe I should see that as a good sign.

Maybe I should ask him if it bothers me so much. I really don't like that idea, because it cements the wrongness of this whole summer. Or because it involves asking Beck about something serious. I'd never get a meaningful response out of him anyway.

When we get everything put back in its place at Blackbridge, the whole place seems to shut down. After evening feedings, I find my cell phone, happy to discover that there's a text from Bri waiting for me.

Travers it is!

I shoot back a quick text to confirm as I stroll into the office to put down my stuff, finding Dad staring off into space. He's balancing the cell phone on its side on the desk, but his eyes are watching the windows. A lick of anxiety runs down my spine with memories of just after Mom left. I found Dad staring off into space a lot back then, like he didn't know what to do with her gone.

I stop in the doorway, and he still doesn't register me.

"Dad?"

That does it, and I'm thankful for that because when he's really off in la la land he'll go minutes without acknowledging he's been asked a question and is expected to respond. This time he looks at me, and tips the phone over until it clatters to a rest. "What's going on?"

He smiles, which for a man who's been staring out the window at nothing is not really what I would call reassuring. It's more of an "I notice you're here, where I'd rather you not be" sort of smile.

"What's wrong?"

"Nothing," he looks at his phone again, and picks it back up. "If you don't mind, sweetie, I'm going to call Belmont and get an update on Star. We're shipping out for Monmouth tomorrow."

I know that. He has this way of repeating information like I haven't known about it for days, or weeks. Like the time he sat Martina and me down to tell us that Mom was staying in California, we both had known well in advance. It was obvious. He tended to do it when there was a situation he didn't know how to handle, in efforts to sweep it away. Downplay and then explain only after the situation and consequences are already common knowledge. It's also a nervous habit. Say something that's obvious when you don't want to say the truth.

Girls, your mother decided to stay with the California tracks for the time being. Instead of *Girls, your mother isn't going to come home.*

Sometimes, I'd appreciate the truth. I watch him speed dial the Belmont barn, and find myself saying, "I think I'll take Kali out."

He nods, barely heard me. I put my bag and cell phone up in the loft, and then thump back down the stairs, actually pissed. Dad should be asking me why I'm not taking out Maggie, or Diver. He should be telling me hell no, I will not be taking a three-year-old filly on a strict training schedule out by myself without a plan. All of this says there's a change coming and it's probably going to suck.

I groom and tack Kali in her stall, then take her outside to mount up and go. After I canter her over the gently rising hills, I ask her to halt.

The filly does it, shifting her hindquarters out in confusion. I think about what I should do with the filly that we haven't done, coming up with a blank. I feel like I've galloped Kali over kingdom come, and nothing good has come from it. After a minute of standing in the incredible heat of the day, I sigh and mutter to the filly, "Screw this, girl."

I reach down and tug at the stirrup leathers until they're dropped several holes. I check to make sure the stirrups are even, and then turn her around, trotting over the even expanse of grass between the hills. If Dad saw this, he wouldn't like it, but it can't hurt and Kali is probably the only horse in the barn that will let me get away with this other than Diver.

I've ridden her nearly every morning for two years, after all. I know what she's capable of.

The space I have to work with isn't exactly ideal, but it works well enough to turn a twenty-meter circle and still have relatively flat ground to ride over. The filly pricks her ears at this new development, turning the circle while I nudge her to the outside, widening and widening until I ask her to do the opposite. It takes her a second to catch on, but she's a smart animal and figures it out, shrinking the circle until I spiral her back out again and break the circle entirely.

I ask her to canter, but she picks the wrong lead. I ask her again, and she gets it right before we turn, looping at the end of the narrow space to double back. She snorts and lowers her head, carrying it by herself instead of using my pressure on the reins to build her own momentum. We go around and around, working our way back to the twenty-meter circle, expanding and shrinking while she rounds almost spontaneously underneath me. My fingers twitch on the reins, and she bobs her head down, plays the bit on her tongue, and keeps shifting out as I ask.

Then finally I break her off the circle and ask her to go. She explodes, gathers herself and plows across the valley with enough momentum to send her up the next hill and over it, then right back down into the next valley before we nearly career right into another horse.

Kali shies so violently I can't even remember staying with her. I just hold on and sit the horse, and I'm glad she makes the right decisions because she slips around a very familiar chestnut with a very enraging blond mane and tail. When Kali comes to a shuttering halt, her chest rising and falling, I whip around and can't help yelling at Beck on Lighter.

"What the hell are you doing?"

I may be screeching, actually. Lighter almost looks gleeful, like this is drama he can work with. Beck, to his credit, looks surprised, but I'm past caring because he's out here where he's not supposed to be, on a horse he's not supposed to be on, and frankly I am so done with this.

"What do you mean what the hell am I doing?" Beck asks, recovering and shifting right into exasperation with me. "You're the one that came down that rise like you had a demon chasing you."

"Because I thought no one else was out here."

"Well, newsflash, Juls. Here I am," he says, and that makes me sit back in the saddle. Beck doesn't even bother looking smug about shutting me up, because it's very plain he's just angry.

"And Dad said you could ride Lighter?" I ask dubiously.

"July, I own Lighter."

"That doesn't answer my question."

He pauses, and I tilt my head at him, knowing the answer.

"Okay, so he didn't say anything about Lighter, but that's really beside the point."

My dissatisfaction with his answer is obvious. "No, it isn't," I say. "Lighter is Lighter, and you're out here by yourself, and you're not even wearing a helmet, Beck. You're asking to get dumped on your head with that colt."

Beck smiles, but it's not like any other smile he's ever given me. This time it's hard. It makes something inside me go very cold.

"Well, July," he says, turning Lighter around and looking at me over his shoulder. "Maybe no one asked you."

A short, disbelieving laugh slips out of my mouth.

Not hours ago we were in a totally different situation. Sure, I was nagging him and he was rolling his eyes, but he was still *Beck* then. This is not Beck. This is some jackass who's taken his place and his horse and appears to have a death wish.

I must tense, because Kali begins to fidget, sliding around to avoid the pressure of my legs. It's a physical effort to lift them off her sides and relax. The filly quiets.

"Why are you acting like this?" I ask. "You know the rules."

He shakes his head. "There aren't any rules right now, Juls."

I have no idea what that means, especially since it's not really Beck's job to be cryptic. He's Beckett Delaney, the smart ass, the second son, the one who's been embracing life and hasn't thought about asking questions. If he'd said he didn't quite care about the rules, it would be normal. This isn't. This is trying my patience.

"What does that even mean?" I ask, because there are always rules. I've been following them for years, and so has he.

"Nothing," he says, shaking his head. I realize he's done with talking to me, which is so unlike him it makes me want to ride Kali over to him so I can punch him and shake him out of it, because this isn't normal. Instead, with everything else so strangely off, I get angry all over again.

"Fine," I say, clipped and finished. "If you want to risk your goddamned life, that's your business."

I tap my legs against Kali's sides and she strides off into an energetic trot, springing past Lighter and Beck, who watch me pass. It's an effort, I can tell, for him to keep Lighter glued to his spot, but he does it impressively enough. As I pass him, I yell back, "Just try not to risk anyone else's while you're at it."

Kali shifts into a canter by herself, and I don't care. I ride it until I'm far out of sight.

Chapter Nine

I don't want to be such a bitch, but it's hard when Beck has suffered a major personality shift in the space of a few hours, Dad is off in some other world, and Martina hangs up on me every time I call. She does it again after I finish up with Kali and climb back into the loft. What am I supposed to do? Sit and stew? Of all the people I can think of, Martina should be interested in what's going on, but instead I find myself picking up my cell and calling Bri.

"What's up?" she asks, and I find it all spilling out before I can stop it. While I'm talking, I realize it sounds like I've turned into some conspiracy theorist, but I don't think I'm wrong. I think something isn't right, and, if anything, this past hour has just made it all blatantly clear.

"I don't know what to say." Bri pauses for a second, and then says, "Can't you ask?"

"Ask who?" I sigh and get up, walking across the loft to my room and falling onto the bed. "No one would tell me anything, even if they had something to say."

"Well, it seems to me that you've got two people to ask."

"My dad is a lost cause," I say, looking at the ceiling. "He can't break bad news until after I've already learned about it. Beck is the one to go to, but if he's going to keep up how he was acting today, there's no way he's telling me anything."

"Then wait," Bri advises. "You don't know, Juls. It could be nothing."

"I suppose," I allow, because it's been made painfully clear to me that regardless of what is going on, I can't do much about it. I could nag Beck half to death, but he'd start to avoid me, and then I'd really be out of options.

"Plus, it's the first day of the meet, right? Don't get too upset too early," Bri says. "What if suddenly everyone shows up tomorrow, or next week? Do you think they'll go to that Haskell thing you were talking about?"

"Maybe," I say. "It's closer to Manhattan, and Quark Star is one of the more important horses in the stable."

"So wait for that," Bri says. "At the very least, wait until after a few big races have come and gone."

I take a breath and nod to myself, and then hear the door to the loft opening. I tell Bri I have to go, but it's just Dad trotting up the stairs. He pauses in the doorway of my room, asks me what I want to order out, and then disappears again.

I hear the shower head turn on. So ends another day.

~~

Monmouth wants to be a park. It's got a big, open grandstand and a newer, enclosed clubhouse. The saddling paddock is shady and populated with trees. There are freshly painted benches, tables with umbrellas. It's no Saratoga, but it tries hard to present itself as clean and family-oriented. For a gambling establishment, that's always hard to pull off.

Quark Star hasn't been at the track long. A few hours, max. We arrived early enough to see him work for the first time over the dirt. The colt has never been to New Jersey, has

97

never been outside of New York, actually, so this is his maiden voyage on a new track. It's important; if he hates the surface, we'll scratch him, stick him back on the van, and trailer him straight to Saratoga, where he likes it. We'll hope we can skip the Haskell entirely and go straight for the Travers.

That option will kind of suck, because if the Haskell isn't Star's race, we've already missed the Jim Dandy yesterday at Saratoga. A nice horse won it, too. A nice horse who will be serious competition in the Travers. I'm really hoping Dad's planning will work out here, because we've stretched ourselves thin in hopes that Star will make up for the most of it.

Jorge is halfway through the colt's morning blow out, this burst of speed meant to sharpen Star for the upcoming race. It's supposed to get Star's game face on, like pushing the go button just long enough and putting on the brakes right when the horse really starts running will frustrate him enough to want to decimate any horse nearby.

It seems to have the desired effect. Star comes off the track quivering, but steady. He's not trying to break away and race around the backside. Jorge jumps to the ground and grins, pats me on the elbow as he walks off and says, "Bet your two dollars on him, lady. To win."

I roll my eyes, but I like his confidence.

"What do you think?" I ask Star, who cranes his head up and dances on the tips of his toes. He's not above some fancy maneuvers on the way back to our rented stall, where only a few members of the press have camped out in a half-hearted effort to get a good look at an up-and-comer. The real media frenzy is a few barns over, where Hot Metal, the Derby and Belmont winner, is parked before the Haskell.

"Want to go see?" Izzie asks conspiratorially while I watch Gus rinse off Star. The big colt has his head turned to the side, like he's listening to something far off and can't quite make it out.

"Go see what?" I ask, rubbing Star's wet muzzle and then wiping the palm of my hand on my jeans.

"Hot Metal," Izzie asks, putting her hands on her hips and shooting me a look like I'm clearly dense. "Who else is there to look at?"

Izzie and I have both seen Hot Metal before, when he was stabled at Belmont a couple of months ago. We walk over to Hot Metal's barn, where a few television cameras and a fleet of photographers are waiting for any glimpse of the horse. We don't get too close, especially since Hot Metal is already out and on display. His groom has the stud chain draped over his nose, because Hot Metal is not exactly a lovable colt. Hot Metal lives up to his name, and he is a giant. In the Belmont Stakes, all he needed to do to make racing room was muscle a few competitors out of the way.

Izzie sighs. She's always had a thing for chestnuts with lots of chrome.

"Thinking of changing employers?" I ask her. She nudges me hard with her hip, and I have to dance over to keep my balance.

"Absolutely not," she says, pushing some of her black and blond hair out her eyes. "He's gorgeous, is all."

Hot Metal turns his white-blazed head and stares us down for a few brief seconds, as if to back up Izzie's opinion with a few arrogant poses. He makes a complete circle around his groom and lowers his head to check out the grass. Before he can take a mouthful of it, he's urged back to stand for the cameras and then led back into the barn.

The show is over. Time to get back to work.

∾

Right before the PA crackles to life and asks us to bring the horses over for the next race, the Haskell Invitational, something normal happens. Laurence and Cynthia Delaney step out of their gleaming Bentley and stroll into the shedrow. It's hard for me to summon up the right reaction, other than awestruck staring.

Really, I didn't expect them at all.

"July," Delaney says with that quiet authority, like he couldn't be convinced to shorten my name like everyone else. He doesn't act much like Beck, although he is tall and broad enough to bring some comparisons to his carefree, if recently insanely moody, offspring. Laurence Delaney probably had that dark and smoldering thing going for him a long time ago, but now his hair is speckled with gray and his neatly trimmed beard is almost entirely white. If I had to describe him in a word, I'd go for patrician. Delaney's whole profile screams out for someone to imitate it in marble.

Cynthia isn't far from the same mark, although she's less strong angles and piercing gaze than she is fair and classically beautiful. I'm pretty sure Jackie O is her idol, because even when she goes riding she looks ready for a fashion shoot.

Delaney strides up with casual grace and brings me in for a hug against his expensive suit, because he has this magnanimous father-figure thing going on, almost to a fault. Cynthia stands nearby and smiles up at Star, who is studying her flopping, feather speckled hat like it might attack him and he's not sure how he will escape this horror by being stuck in a stall.

I don't have much room to move my arms, being pinned down to my sides by Delaney's hug, so I manage to lift one hand and pat his elbow, both as a hello and as an indicator that he can let go of me now.

He releases me. Behind him, I see Beck's little sister Olivia hovering near the door. Her too short summer dress and heels make her look like she's striving to appear older than she really is, and she's mainly succeeding. Her professionally highlighted mouse brown hair looks like it's never been ruffled by breeze, but her nails are chewed down to the quick. I smile at her, and she tentatively smiles back, but stays where she is in the doorway. After a minute she pulls out her cell phone and disappears altogether.

Another sleek car pulls up next to the Bentley. Initially I think it's Beck come equipped with a new toy, but it turns out to be none other than Matthew Delaney. He unfolds out of the car and adjusts the jacket of his suit, aviators shielding his eyes. If anyone inherited Delaney's looks, it's Matt. I give the sight of him a curious stare, wondering why he's here instead of his brother, because Matt is about as sentimental about this sport as he is with anything else, and as far as I can tell that would be with nothing at all.

"So where's your father?" Delaney asks, turning to study Quark Star. Cynthia has the colt by the halter and is stroking one manicured hand down the front of his face. Star nuzzles at the hem of her dress, and Cynthia coos at him, stepping out of the way before he tries to take a bite of the slippery material.

"In the office," I say. "We'll need to report to the paddock in a few minutes."

Delaney nods, pulls a toothpick out of his pocket and begins to chew on it thoughtfully while he watches his horse. "How are things at the farm shaping up?"

I consider that for a minute, wondering what he could possibly want to know that Beck hasn't been telling him. What my father hasn't been telling him.

"Fine," I say automatically, while Matt wanders into the stable. "They're fine."

Delaney smiles. "I heard you were riding that Kaliningrad filly the other day. Seems like a good thing to do," he says, like it's almost thoughtless, although I know it's not. "Giving her something else to think about might do her some good."

I narrow my eyes at him, wondering just what Beck *has* been saying, but Dad appears, and they're lost in the conversation of horses. Cynthia pulls me away, leads me right out of the shedrow altogether and says, "Let's go down ahead of them, July. Let the men have their discussion."

That's not really how I do things, but I go along. Matt nods to us wordlessly and stays with the men, talking about manly things, I guess. Olivia is by the Bentley, rapidly texting on her phone.

"Olivia Delaney," Cynthia says, taking her daughter's arm and steering her away from the car. "Put the phone away and come with us."

Olivia shoots me a tight smile. She throws the phone into her bag and shakes loose from Cynthia's hand, taking a few exaggerated steps ahead of us and marching with purpose down to the saddling paddock. Her dress swishes dangerously across the back of her thighs. It's almost amusing to me, even though I catch the look Cynthia gives Olivia's back. This mother-daughter push and pull routine is fascinating from an outsider perspective.

"I really miss Blackbridge this time of year," Cynthia says after a minute. I expect her to say something more specific, but she sighs and smiles at me. "I don't even know what to do with myself in Manhattan right now."

She laughs, and I don't know what to say. There is, of course, the most nagging thought. Might as well. "Are you coming up to Saratoga this year?"

Cynthia looks at me, weighing her options. "Possibly," she says. "Laurence and I might if we find a moment to escape. If I can't bear the city another day, I definitely will. I know Olivia likes it, though. She's such a Manhattanite."

Truer words were never spoken. I don't know what to take from any of this; Cynthia is at best a perfect socialite. She knows exactly what to say to turn a hazy situation even hazier. So I smile and we walk the rest of the way.

"I'm surprised to see Matt here," I say, just because the curiosity is eating at me. "I was expecting Beck."

Cynthia pauses again before she answers, her fluidity flawed by the hesitation it takes for her to formulate a response. "Matt's been taking a greater interest in the farm this summer, and you can imagine how happy Laurence is about that. Beck decided to stay in the city this time."

Bull.

"He's looking forward to this race, but you know how he is, July," Cynthia says breezily, waving her hand. "Beck hasn't had a care in the world since he began drawing breath."

That smacks of truth, but the way I left him in the galloping lanes the other day would indicate that we're all a bit wrong where it concerns Beck. I bite the inside of my cheek and tell myself not to bring anything else up.

It's only a few more minutes before Dad and Delaney show up with Gus, Quark Star strolling along like he owns the place. Matt brings up the rear, his aviators hiding what is surely intense focus on his cell phone. The only person missing from our party is Beck. It's like we can't ever get back to normal this summer.

I stop by Quark Star's stall after he's led inside. Dad starts tacking him up, while Gus keeps the colt occupied. I'm not stationary more than a couple of seconds before Matt walks right into me and drops his phone, which is open to his e-mail. Talk about scary focus.

"Never check your e-mail and walk at the same time," I advise him, picking up his phone and handing it back to him. He and Beck have the same smile, a kind of effortless appeal.

Matt slips the phone into his pocket. "I'll try to remember that. How's life, Juls?"

"The same," I shrug, which is not true at all, but then Matt doesn't need to know how concerned I am. Matt is like a steel vault, and no family secrets are coming out of him any time soon. "Are you coming to Saratoga this year?"

That's an easy question. The answer is no, because he never comes to Saratoga ever.

"Maybe," he says, which is yet another answer that makes me want to scream. What is with these people and their weirdness this year? It's like the world has been turned upside down.

"Really," I say, clearly not believing him. He chuckles at my tone, and shrugs.

"What can I say?" he asks. "I'm nostalgic for a simpler time."

"I don't think Saratoga was ever simple," I say.

"Not with Martina around," he agrees. "How's your sister?"

"Not at Saratoga."

"Didn't think so," he says. "You know, I heard she works in my part of the city and briefly entertained the idea of asking her out to lunch."

"And then you stopped yourself when you realized that was a horrible idea?" I lift an eyebrow, hardly able to stop myself.

"Pretty much," he says. "I put down the phone when I realized she probably still wanted to eviscerate me."

"She'll get over it eventually," I say, although she probably won't. I'm still not clear on what went wrong with Matt and Martina. They began dating right after Mom left, or doing something that resembled dating, anyway. After the better part of a year Martina dropped him like a rock and moved on, but not until she got in a few choice insults and told me men were all dicks. I decided that was enough of an explanation.

Matt pulls a face and says, "Martina doesn't get over anything."

I think about that for a minute and say, "You're right."

"So no phone calls with the ex," he shrugs. "Which reminds me that Beck said something about needing to talk to you."

A sick rush of confusion floods through me, and all I say is, "Huh?"

"Yeah," Matt shrugs. "Said something about you being pissed at him? I figured that was pretty much par for the course around here. If you or Martina weren't pissed at me or my idiot brother the world might end."

"Oh," I say, my confusion constricting right into anger with Beck. His attitude and his absence suck, and I realize I'm going to have to yell at him. If it's over the phone, so be it. "Well, I am pissed at him. He's a jerk."

"Yeah, I know," Matt says with sympathy. "But we're required to love him anyway."

His phone begins to chime from his pocket, and he gives me a brotherly nudge in the shoulder as he walks off to take his call.

I slip away from the gathering at Quark Star's stall, winding through the horses and clumps of people to find a deserted spot under one of the trees. I pull out my cell and find Beck's number, knowing even as I do it that I really shouldn't. I should remain pissed at him and save it for later, so yelling at him will be more satisfying. Calling him feels like I'm playing right into his hands, but I'm too curious for my own good. That's it, I tell myself. Curiosity killed the cat.

"There's the phone call I was waiting for," he says when he picks up. I make a face into the phone.

"Yeah, so we've got almost everyone in attendance here except for you," I say, hearing the telling sounds of the city through the phone. "What's going on, Beck?"

"Admittedly? Very little. It's a nice change."

"What does that mean?" I ask, my frustration starting to flow. It's maddening to have this feeling that everyone is in on the same secret and that you are the one person that can't be in the know. He doesn't say anything.

"Nothing at all, huh? Well, at least do us some measure of respect by watching the race."

"Yeah, give my best wishes to Star," he says. His voice is muffled by sounds of traffic, someone leaning on a car horn. I know that he's not going to make any promises about watching the race. He pauses, and neither of us speaks. New York noise keeps flooding through the phone, riding along on my increasing sense of uncertainty.

"You wanted to talk to me, remember?"

"Did I?" he asks. My fingers clench just a fraction tighter around the phone.

"What the hell is going on, Beck?" I ask, feeling like I might explode if I don't scream the question out loud. I'm only met with silence.

Finally, like he's gone through all his options and has settled on the right words, he says, "I'm just not feeling familial today, Juls. See you in Saratoga."

And he has the nerve to hang up. I stare at the phone in utter confusion, wondering what bit him in the ass. I have the itching compulsion to call him back and yell at him, but I don't want to give him that sort of control. I'll have plenty of time to yell at him later, in theory. So I fight every urge in my body, and put the phone away.

The race is beautiful, but we don't win. Hot Metal stalks the pace all the way through, and Quark Star practically hitches a ride alongside and just behind him. Hot Metal flies forward at the right time, and Jorge has no choice but to go with him, so the two horses are alone in the front of the pack when they race down the homestretch. Hot Metal tries to shake Star off several times, leaping forward and digging down and coming up with more in each stride, and Star matches him perfectly all the way to the end.

It's the matter of a head bob that doesn't go our way, and the rest of the field is eight lengths behind. When I watch the horses slow down in the first turn, it feels like someone's punched me hard in the stomach, because it's hard to draw a full breath. I've screamed myself hoarse. Even Olivia looks stunned, because she manages a shaky smile that's either for real or for the cameras that may be on her.

I doubt they're on her. We haven't won. The whooping and hollering further down the grandstand belongs to Hot Metal's connections, and I try not to feel a stab of regret underneath the sheer glee over how awesome our colt is. He was there right to the end.

"Looks like the Travers?" Delaney asks no one in particular. Dad nods.

∿

We take Quark Star directly to Blackbridge after the race, after he's cool and clean. His new stall is located almost directly underneath my bed. I shove my phone in the back pocket of my jeans as I work, because even if I'm not really expecting a phone call, I'm expecting a phone call. That might not make much sense, but I guess I can file it under stupidity or hope and not feel bad when the phone call never materializes.

All through evening feeding, the phone doesn't ring. Through dinner, the phone doesn't ring. When it's finally dusk, just barely light enough to see, the phone still doesn't ring. It's only the arrival of headlights on the farm drive, when I accept that the phone is not going to ring.

Instead, Beck parks his car outside the main training barn. I see him from my place on the balcony. Because one of the barn lights shines all the way down the wall, he can see me as if I'm standing in the middle of the afternoon sun.

"Hey," he says up to me.

"You're an asshole," I greet him, and he smiles.

"That's been said," he says, pushing his hands into his pockets and looking up. His legs are slightly bowed, and you can see it in the way the lights cast his shadow down onto the gravel. I lean into the wooden railing and cross my arms, waiting for more. "Actually," he continues, "I think you've said that a few times yourself."

"I don't think I could count the number of names I've called you," I agree.

He nods, looks down at the gravel, and then back up at me. "You want to come down?"

"Are you going to apologize?"

"I was planning on some sort of explanation, yes."

"But no apology."

"I haven't been known to really give those, remember?"

"This is why you're an asshole."

"Twice in one night," he says, nodding like this is impressive. "Think you can make it three?"

"I think that's well within my reach," I say, and then sigh. "Fine. I'll be down in a sec."

I take my time finding my flip-flops. It is absurdly hot, even at night, and I've finally caved to wearing shorts when there's no chance I'm going to be working a horse moderately hard in the near future. I hate wearing shorts, because my legs are so deathly pale. It's the price you pay for wearing jeans most of your life.

I slip out of the loft and try to keep the slapping flip-flops quiet on the way down to the barn. Beck is leaning against his car, this old Mustang that would be nice if he bothered to put any time into it at all, which he doesn't. I will say this for the Delaneys: they don't exactly shower their kids with luxury items. The Mustang is a hand-me-down from Matt, and Olivia hasn't shown any interest in driving from what I can see.

Of course, keeping a car in Manhattan is in itself a luxury. So maybe I'm wrong.

"This better be good," I say, stopping in front of him. He relaxes against the side of the car, considers me for a minute. He looks horrible, like he's been working too hard. The only thing is that Beck doesn't work. His shirt is dirty laundry pile worthy and is halfheartedly tucked into the front of jeans torn at the hems.

"That depends on what your definition of 'good' is," he says, watching me with this steady, quiet air that I find unnerving. Beck doesn't do steady and quiet, pretty much ever.

"How about you tell me what's going on, and we'll determine if it's worthy of freaking out?"

He laughs, like that's actually funny. I wait him out, concern simmering in my stomach, until he sobers up, leans against the car and rubs a hand through his hair. I think he'd rather not tell me when he starts talking.

"You know that scheme that was reported last month? The guy with thirty something watches?"

I cannot believe he remembers that detail. This doesn't sound good, but I nod.

"My dad knows the guy."

What do you say to that? "Oh," is the only reaction that claws its way up my throat, followed by, "So what does that mean?"

"The short story," he says, "is that my dad's investment firm put money where it should have been profitable and now that money is gone."

"How much money is gone?"

"You know how many investors were screwed over in this scheme?" he asks me, like I keep up with this sort of thing. I barely read the news. If it's not horse racing, or the racing programs I scan for Mom's name, I'm pretty much content in the dark. Truth be told, I was lucky to see that broadcast about any of this when I did, or I'd be totally ignorant right now.

"Couldn't say."

"There were hundreds," Beck informs me. "And our firm was kind of the largest client."

"Oh."

My voice is tiny, like the smallest Smurf being given the worst news.

Beck smiles down at his shoes, because for him there's just enough dark humor to be found in my one-syllable responses. This isn't fair of him, because for me it feels like the ground is tilting out from under my feet. I stop myself, grimacing, because I have to wonder which of us this will hurt more. I have to know how much this will hurt, period.

"That's why I wasn't at Star's race," he says. "It's why I haven't been acting myself. It's just that I'm so incredibly . . . pissed."

"What does this mean?" I ask, feeling ridiculously stupid. I still have to ask.

Beck lifts his gaze to my face. He's been staring at my legs, probably because they are so brilliant and blinding. "It means we're all going to have to give something up."

I don't know what to say to that, because it seems like any answers he'd give are obvious. Something means the farm, the horses, Dad, and me. All in one go. It might not happen so swiftly, but it will happen nevertheless.

"You say you're pissed, but you seem very calm about this," I say.

"So do you," he replies.

"Well, I'm not."

He nods.

"Anyway," he says, lifting himself off the car. A cold wave of panic washes over me, like he's leaving and he can't go now that he's told me all of this, even when he probably can't answer all of the questions that are threatening to spill out of my mouth. "There's going to be this article in the *New York Times* tomorrow. Nothing I haven't told you, but I wanted you to know before you read it."

I'm wondering if Dad knows anything about this. He probably does. Of course he does, because this would be history repeating itself again. It's my turn to nod.

"And for the record," he sighs, pulling his keys from his pocket. "I'm sorry I'm a dick."

He doesn't follow it up with anything. Not a word. It occurs to me that I'm a horrible person for not trying harder to figure out the problem, for getting angry like I usually do.

"Accepted," I say in a small voice, barely my own. I want to say more, but he doesn't let me. He's in his car and I turn back toward the barn.

When he drives back to the main house, I watch the lines of the car blur and disappear into the dark. I wonder how long he's known. I wonder how long we have left.

Chapter Ten

I'm not playing around when I spread the newspaper open on the kitchen table. I've gotten tired of playing dumb. So I've resorted to this.

I smooth down the crease in the middle of the black and gray print. There, right in the middle of the first page, is the article that consists of a lengthy investigation into the investments and clients of the so-called Hines-Clifton scheme. I don't read the whole thing. Actually, I skim it until I see Laurence Delaney's name and his firm. I nearly choke when I see the dollar figure sitting there in the same sentence. Beck really wasn't kidding.

I leave the paper there, and watch from the kitchen counter as Dad walks right by it and goes for the coffee.

"Big day, huh kid?"

I stare at him, because quite honestly I am amazed.

"Sure," I say after a minute, feigning a smile. "Absolutely."

He fixes himself some toast and leaves the loft before he can do something like sit me down and say, "Okay, July, here's what's happened and this is what we're going to do about it." Because that would naturally be too easy, right? I walk over to the table and stare down at the paper, realizing that I am no better, but I'm not the one who makes the decisions here. I'm not the one that has to push for them. I don't always have to be the one to face down every bill, head injury and financial disaster, do I?

The paper is really the only answer I've got, and I don't like it. I fold it back up and throw it in the recycling bin on my way out of the loft. Dad is right—it is a big day. Our wonder filly, Galaxy Collision, will run against colts for the first time in her career, and Lighter is running for the first time. I've got a bet to settle.

~~~

"So I'm thinking," Beck says, leaning against the side of the stall while Dad tightens Galaxy's overgirth and I stand in the shade, relishing the slight breeze that drifts through the paddock every now and then. I give Beck a suspicious sideways glance.

"Shocking," I deadpan, and he smiles.

"Oh, July," he sighs. "Sarcasm is just a defense mechanism, you know."

"Did you learn that in some freshman psych class?"

"No," he says, "I really don't have much of an interest in human psychology. Really, what's the point beyond learning everyone else is wrong and you're always right?"

"You might want to rethink that," I point out. "It sort of has a self-absorbed wrongness to it."

He smiles and continues. "I think we might want to sweeten the pot."

"Absolutely not." I put my foot down.

"Oh, come on. This isn't an interesting bet, Juls. What happens as a result? One of us gets our head kicked in, right? Where's the fun in that? Where's the challenge?"

"One of us gets to feel smug and satisfied while the other one acknowledges how stupid he is," I say, feeling quite smug and satisfied already.

"I noticed what you did there," Beck says.

"Oh, yeah? Pretty astute of you."

"You ever wonder what will happen when I get tired of your abuse?"

"Please," I say, unimpressed. "As if that would ever happen."

The path we've taken to get Lighter to his maiden race this afternoon isn't exactly epic, and he hasn't done anything so horrible as to get banned from the track. To Beck's delight, he passed his gate tests with flying colors, and didn't act like a total loon when we trained him in the saddling paddock, so it must mean he's at least ready to run.

Running straight, keeping a jockey on his back and winning will be another story. He's already dumped Pilar in his second to last work, and while I haven't fallen off of him recently, it's only a matter of time.

The call for riders up comes, and Dad boosts Jorge into the saddle. Galaxy Collision goes sashaying into line, her perfectly combed and conditioned jet-black tail swishing over her hind legs as she goes. There are five colts in the race, and her, the only filly. She doesn't look like a filly to anyone who couldn't tell the horses apart by a glance. She looks like a colt-crushing monster. I keep my eyes on her, watching her parade around the enclosure with her white-striped head held low, stepping under herself and stretching the muscles over her top line.

She's getting ready to run.

When she and Jorge disappear under the stands, we climb up to our seats. Delaney isn't here today. That's not too shocking now. Although the Whitney is traditionally a televised race and today is made even more of a media circus by the fact that the undefeated, Eclipse Award-winning filly is going to take a shot at it, he leaves it to Beck and stays enclosed in Manhattan.

You can hear the whispers sometimes, and see the pitying faces. At least, I perceive them as pitying, because I wouldn't know what else to call them. As far as I know, Blackbridge is the only one to make this fatal error.

The horses glide into the starting gate. They're older, more professional than the two-year-olds that will arrive on the scene in the next race, so when the last horse is in line it's only a handful of seconds before they're released onto the track.

Clean break, good start. Galaxy Collision streams up with the leaders and dashes across the track, snagging onto the second position behind the leader. She'll sit there, content to stalk the whole way around. The crowd murmurs, anxious for the result.

The great thing about racing a filly against the boys is the immediate cheering section the filly gathers, almost by default. There are too many posters to count proclaiming anything from *Girl Power* to *Galaxy Rules*, and a girl is almost always holding them with a hopeful grin on her face.

I want Galaxy to win for more than those smiles. She deserves it all on her own, and I can't help the death grip I have on the metal bar in front of me when the horses spill into the final turn.

"Come on, Galaxy," I hear Beck say under his breath next to me. "That's it, girl."

I don't register saying the same things, but I am. It's like you can't help the words that stream out of your mouth, because the race means so much and the filly running in it is too special for words.

Galaxy Collision changes leads, and you could miss it easily if you weren't looking for it. She begins to drive, putting away the tiring frontrunner and grasping the lead with a tenacity that I know is not going to flag. Her ears flick once, twice, and Jorge taps her on her flank with his crop to remind her to keep her head on business, but she doesn't need it. No one is close.

The filly blows them all away.

When I come back to myself, I'm screaming. I'm bouncing up and down next to Beck, and his arm is around my waist because it's second nature to reach out and grab something during the race. To grab it and hold on, or shake it, or just feel that it's there and you can steady yourself against it to bring yourself back to earth when the race is done.

I turn to him and grin, reach up and wrap an arm around his neck without thinking to drag him into a hug. His arms press around me and I keep bouncing. We shake together, while the filly comes back home.

~~

"It's good luck, you know," Beck says while we watch Lighter bound around his outrider like a particularly flighty bimbo who can't comprehend why he's being held back from racing straight to the starting gate.

"What's good luck?" I ask, watching the blond chestnut toss his head up and down, dancing his hindquarters from side to side until he's bumping against his pony to the point where they're both walking sideways across the track. I really hope this isn't a horrible idea.

"A win earlier in the day . . ."

"That really only pertains to jockeys," I remind him, because Jorge rides our big horses. Our Galaxy Collisions. Pilar rides our lesser-known horses as she works through her year-long apprenticeship.

"Still," he says, and slips his hand behind my neck, kneading the extremely tense muscles there. A whole shiver builds under his hand and shoots down my spine, shocking me so much I pull away. I immediately tell myself to forget it, that it's nothing, but my stomach and heart disagree with me. "It's good luck," he insists, ignoring the few inches of space I've put between us. He drops his hand to his side. "Still want to go forward with this bet?"

"Of course," I say, because we both know luck has nothing to do with this.

When Lighter gets to the gate, I know he's eyeing the thing like he still doesn't know quite what to make of it. That's a two-year-old issue that he'll get over after a few experiences where nothing horrible happens and he breaks clean. He goes in after an insistent tug from the assistant starter, and when they're released onto the track there are ten two-year-olds playing bumper cars before realizing that there's a whole track in front of them.

The colts make a mad dash for the expanse of dirt, and I notice Lighter's shocking pale mane zip along the outside of the group. Pilar sits easy on him, doing no more than guid-

119

ing. I see Beck's silks, a take on Blackbridge's black and white scheme, only in reverse, flashing through the group as Lighter goes flying to the front on the far turn.

The race is short, but Lighter doesn't seem to care about strategy. Pilar knows better than to try hauling him around the course, so he goes skipping down the middle of the track with all systems go.

Beck laughs when the colt pulls away from the group. I don't really know what to do when no one can muster a challenge, leaving the whole race to Lighter as he goes gallivanting past the finish line without having been touched with the crop.

That little jerk. I watch Pilar persuade him to slow down in the first turn, and Lighter is slow in accepting this part of the process. His head is up, and he's responding about as well as he does any other day, which means he'll get around to slowing when he feels like it. It takes the approach of an outrider to knock some sense into the colt, so I'm mainly shaking my head at this while Beck does this enthusiastic dance next to me. Even Dad is pretty happy, his eyes lighting up in a way that tells me one thing: we've got a potential Derby prospect.

In the space of a minute, Lighter has gone from dense hothead to one of the most important horses in the barn. I would bet all the money I have in my small checking account that he'll run in a stakes race next, right here at Saratoga.

"So, Juls." Beck is done celebrating, or has at least finished the initial shock of victory. I know how he operates, and he's nowhere near done with this. Now it is time to be infinitesimally frustrating by rubbing my face in how right he was, because it's never how wrong I am with Beck. He just likes it when he's always right, hence why he's never really apologized at any point in his life. Except that once.

"Yes, Beck?"

"How right was I?"

"You're halfway there," I allow, but he's still grinning up a storm, his whole being alive, too thrilled to head down to meet his horse because he needs to revel first. "I'm thinking how sad everyone will be now that you're no longer going to be providing comic relief in the mornings."

"Oh," he says, like I'm serious about this. "I'm still showing up in the mornings. How else am I supposed to glory in watching you ride Lighter?"

"I hope you know that if Lighter kills me, I am blaming you."

"I'll keep that in mind," he nods, but he's got that spark in his eyes and I can't keep making this about losing a bet, not when it's Lighter and Beck. So while we're walking down the stairs to the first level, headed to meet Pilar and the colt, I lean my shoulder against his arm. He takes this as an order to move, but I press closer until he gets it. He looks down at me, surprised. Some part of me doesn't feel very good about that.

"Congratulations," I say, and some of that tenseness loosens in him. He puts an arm around me and squeezes tight.

～ぃ

When we get down to the winner's circle, Pilar is all jubilation. Dad hugs her after the photos, mindless of the dirt she has smeared all over her silks. Gus leads Lighter back to the stables, and Pilar takes the saddle to weigh back in, still grinning for all she's worth. If there's any justice in this world,

Dad will keep her on for Lighter's next race, which would be her biggest break yet.

Lighter is at least tired afterward, because he doesn't act up when we load him onto the trailer with Galaxy Collision and take them back to Blackbridge. He doesn't even do anything awful when we unload them and settle them back into their stalls. I stand for a moment in front of Lighter's stall, watching him kick around his bedding and then shove his nose into the fresh hay net that hangs near the door. I realize that I could get to like this Lighter, but I'm not holding my breath.

The colt blows out a throaty nicker, and I leave him to his hay. It's been a good day at Saratoga, better than most, and when Izzie and Pilar come down the aisle there isn't an option when it comes to what they're proposing.

"We're going to Rustic," Izzie says, grabbing my hands and spinning around. "You have to come with us."

"Sure," I say, dancing around Izzie and slipping out of her grasp. "Just let me put on better shoes."

She nods emphatically at my manure-encrusted boots. "Hurry up. We're meeting Gus there."

"Yes," Pilar says, grinning at Izzie. "God knows we can't hold up Izzie when Gus is involved."

"It's called being polite," Izzie says as I head for the loft to change into something that isn't caked in barn dust.

"It's called overactive hormones," I hear Pilar snark back at Izzie, who screeches something I don't make out while I let myself into the loft and bend over to unlace my boots, kicking them off into the corner. I notice my phone on the kitchen counter, and realize I didn't have it the whole day. There is a missed call from Martina, but no voicemail. I decide to let it go, and hunt down my shoes. More than likely she didn't mean to call me in the first place.

Rustic is an old brewpub, more bar than restaurant. Pilar and I can sit around in it all night without anyone kicking us out for being underage. It also helps that I've been coming here since I was twelve. The owner knows who I am through Dad, who used to lead more of a social life back with Mom, so I tend to always show up here in August.

When we get there, Gus is already at a booth by the window. There's a pitcher of beer waiting for Izzie, and soda for me and Pilar. I slide in next to Pilar, while Izzie sticks herself close to Gus and reaches for the beer.

"Is there a better way to cap off the first week at Saratoga?" Izzie asks.

"Not that I know of," Pilar grins. "Except for that nasty bankruptcy business."

"That," Gus nods sagely, rotating his beer in its spot on the table. "Bad business all around."

"Nothing's happened yet," I chime in, preferring to be the bringer of optimism to a group of people who are decidedly more realistic than I am for the time being. I know how they feel. In any normal situation, I'd be right there with them. I don't want to take anything going on as real quite yet.

"More or less true," Izzie says. "Galaxy and Lighter won today, and Pilar may have a mount for the Hopeful after all. Drink up, ladies and gentleman."

"What do you mean about the Hopeful?" I ask.

"I want Pilar to ride him," Beck says from behind me, and I whip around, nearly catching his face with the back of my head. He jerks back and smiles down at me from his perch on the booth behind me. "Hey, July."

"What are you doing here?" I ask, eyeing the beer he's balancing on the back of the seat. Of course he would have some fake ID. I look behind him, noticing a few of the people that were with him the first day of the meet. They're carrying on some conversation by themselves, but the willowy platinum blonde he's sitting next to has her head craned around, watching us with interest.

"Lighter is going to run in the Hopeful next month," Beck informs me, crossing his arms over the back of the bench seat and resting his chin on them. "That's why. But you know, Juls, we could make the Hopeful more interesting . . ."

"No," I blurt out immediately, and he laughs.

"Maybe we could go for something small, like an admission of wrongness on your part," he says. "Maybe an apology?"

"You can forget it," I tell him flatly. "Lighter may have won a maiden . . ."

"By daylight," Izzie points out behind me, and I give her a look that she shrugs at.

"But that doesn't mean I'm saying I'm wrong. Besides, Beck, I'm riding him for the rest of the meet. I think that's enough."

"Maybe I'd let you out of that," Beck says thoughtfully, "if you apologized."

"I'm not doing any such thing." He can forget it. Jackass.

"Fine," Beck says, lifting himself off of the back of the chair and putting some space between us, suddenly making it apparent how close we were to begin with. I blink at him, and lift my chin in that stubborn way Beck knows I'm good at. "When Pilar wins the Hopeful, I'm sure you'll come around."

Pilar brightens at this, because we all know what she's thinking—it could only be a whim that Beck's insisting she ride Lighter. Tomorrow, he could change his mind. Maybe he could go all of August thinking Pilar, only to change to Jorge at the last minute. Either way, I know he'll get an excellent rider. Beck knows it, too. And he'll make the decision for his horse, not for Jorge or Pilar, no matter how hard they've worked for us.

"You keep thinking that," I tell him with a cheerful smile. He leans down again, close enough that the blond girl beside him starts to look anxious.

"Oh, I will," he grins down at me. "Don't celebrate too hard, July."

Then he pops back over to his side of the bench seat, saying something I can't hear that makes the blond laugh. When I turn back around, Gus and Izzie are grinning like idiots. Pilar is in her own world, staring at her soda like it has some answers about her future. I feel warm inside, because talking about the Hopeful is so much better than thinking about everything else.

I'd have to thank Beck for that.

Chapter Eleven

us drops me off outside the training barn, and I immediately know something is wrong. The horses and the barn are fine—it's the fact that Martina's very recognizable, cherry red Honda is sitting right next to my car that tips me off.

I stand there for a second, not sure what to do or what I'll be walking into when I arrive in the loft. Dad is almost certainly asleep. I check my watch just to be sure, as if it's going to tell me something other than after midnight. Dad hasn't stayed up after midnight at any point I can remember, and there is almost no chance he'd wake up if Martina just happened to stroll in the front door. I've got enough experience with this, I think. She's been tromping through the house at all hours of the night and waking up no one except me since she was in high school.

Ultimately, I don't have much of a choice. I have to walk up to the loft eventually, and I know Martina is waiting for me. Falling right onto my bed and sleeping in my clothes is not going to be an option tonight.

The door to the loft is open, and just as I suspected, Martina is sitting on the sofa. A bottle of wine sits nearby on the floor and the television is set at a whisper in front of her. There's a box of Kleenex on the coffee table, half the box in wads around her and on the floor. There's also a mug in front of her, probably because all of our drinking glasses are dirty.

The whole thing is a predictable romantic comedy that's heavy on the melodrama.

"Martina?" I ask the room, and she looks up at me. Her face is red. Her hair's a tumbled, fashionable mess. She's wearing a dotted blouse and denim trousers. A floral print, short-sleeved jacket is still belted around her waist. If anything, her bright blue eyes are even more clear and beautiful, because Martina somehow manages to look good even through a catastrophic bender.

"July!" She stands up and then sits back down, deciding instead to pat the sofa next to her, beckoning me closer.

"Martina," I sigh, sinking slowly onto the sofa. She buries her face in her hands.

"I called," she says, like this is supposed to explain something. "I called and no one answered."

"I forgot my phone," I say in lieu of an apology. I don't feel like it, because I am not the one who has been answering the phone and hanging up for no reason. "Why are you here?"

Martina says, "You were right, you know."

"About what?"

"About avoiding men altogether."

"I don't avoid men," I say. "Did you come up here because of Scott?"

"You never liked Scott, did you?" Martina asks suddenly.

I shrug. "I never really knew Scott."

"You were always never around," Martina says, going for the mug and downing the rest of the contents. I watch her finish it off, and then feel bad about not stopping her when she fills the mug up again. She shakes the last few drops out of the bottle, and I really hope that's the only one she brought with her because at least this means she's finished for the night.

"You could say we've got different priorities," I try.

Martina snorts at that, an old laugh she's valiantly stamped out of existence unless she's drunk. The laughter dies right there, and she stares down at the mug she cradles between her hands. "I broke up with Scott."

"I know."

"He was being an asshole," she says. "He bought a ring and everything."

This is a new one. Usually Martina goes after the kind of boys who don't exactly scream commitment. It's one of her built-in safety features. If she doesn't like him, which is usually the case after a few weeks, she cuts them loose, and in the long run there's usually no question that this is where it would have wound up anyway.

Scott was different from the beginning. From the few times I met him, he had white picket fence, two cats and a dog written all over him. How he saw the same qualities in Martina is anyone's guess, although I suppose that's just it. Maybe he never saw them to begin with.

"He proposed." Martina huffs down at her wine, lifting it up to her lips and taking a large gulp. I wince, for her and the wine.

"What's the big deal?"

"I just turned twenty-one," she says loudly, and I shush her to no avail. "I need to go to college, July. I need to not be pinned down, have a job that I hate, have a boyfriend with stupid ideas."

"All very true."

"I need to not have a boyfriend," Martina says, going for a sip this time instead of a healthy swallow. "So now I have no boyfriend."

"Mission accomplished."

She smiles at me. A big, red wine-stained smile.

"Is there something else?" I ask, prodding.

"Oh," she says, swaying into me with that smile going full force. "I quit my job."

Fantastic. Dad will love that.

"Why?"

"It's not in the new plan."

"So what are you going to do?"

"I came here," she says with a shrug. "It smells."

"Okay," I say, watching her down the rest of the wine and almost miss the coffee table trying to put the mug back. I grab it and watch as she falls limply onto the sofa, giggling like there's something really funny about this. Her dark hair tumbles across her face.

"Stay there."

She waves at me, and I roll my eyes. I put the mug in the sink and set the wine bottle in the recycling bin. Martina is lucky that the third room is still set up, because otherwise she'd be sleeping on the sofa tonight. I come back over to the sofa and snag her hands, but it's like trying to move dead weight.

"Martina," I say, nudging her sharply in the leg. "Help me out here."

"Where are we going?"

"Your old room."

She sighs, like this is going to be a real effort on her part. Otherwise she makes no real move to lift herself off the sofa.

"Look," I snap at her. "You decided to come up here, so it's either the sofa or the bed. I figure you'd like the bed. If you throw up, it's at least contained to your space, and you have to clean it up."

"Were you ever anything other than Mom?" Martina asks, narrowing eyes. "Because you suck at being her."

"Mom sucked at being her."

For some reason, Martina thinks this is really funny and she giggles again. I want to leave her there in frustration, but that's not acceptable. I pull on her hand and she finally sits up to allow me to steer her toward her bedroom. I get her to the bed and she crawls over it, curling up against the stale pillows and instantly falling asleep. One of her beautiful leather pumps falls off and rolls to the carpeted floor.

I frown at it, and then give in to the impulse to pull the other one off her foot, sticking both by the bedside table so she won't lose them. There's a quilt at the foot of the bed, so I pull it over her and turn off the light. Her form becomes nothing more than a large lump in the middle of the bed, hard to see and discern as my sister.

I close the door.

∿

I'm finishing up with Diver the next morning when I notice that Dad is watching me closely. I mentally check Diver, making sure he's not stepping funny, but he's his normal easy self. So I pull him up next to Dad. "What?"

"Martina is going to help out around here this month," he says. I nod, accepting this. Martina may not look it, but she's groomed plenty of horses. She's iced and wrapped enough Thoroughbred legs for a lifetime.

Dad looks back down at his tablet, like this is all that needs to be said. I look at him expectantly, and he sighs.

"Starting tomorrow," he adds to his statement, and I have to laugh about that. The last I saw Martina, she was still snoring in bed where I left her.

"Go on, July," he tells me, shooing me off. "Get Diver cooled off. We've got races today, and no time."

"Story of our lives," I say to him, turning Diver on the forehand and tapping him into a trot, heading for the gap. When I get him rinsed off and settled happily back into his stall, I hear rustling in the office and find Martina staring at the coffee maker as it spits into her coffee mug.

"Welcome back to the land of the living," I tell her and she scowls at me over her shoulder. "Are you ready to be put to work? I have a few jobs in mind."

"Don't start with me today, July," she warns me, turning back to the coffee maker.

I guess sisterly bonding is off the table now that she's sober, but who am I kidding? Working with the horses is the last thing she wants to do. If she's lucky, Dad will put her to work as farm secretary. No one knows how to organize an office like she does. If she's unlucky, she'll be out on the track with me, that frown permanently following me around.

Great. Just great.

I push away from the office door and turn around. Kali is stabled across the way, and she has her head sticking out of her stall. She's giving me that look, which I interpret as *take me out of here and let's go.*

I go.

I'm breaking a lot of rules. I take Kali out, which is broken rule number one. I don't tell anyone, broken rule number two. I don't really care what Dad's plans are for Kali's training, which is broken rule number three, and probably the worst one overall. We ride out to the empty galloping lanes behind the training oval, but I still don't have much interest in riding the filly at a breakneck pace.

Instead I halt her and take a glance around. Kali does the same, working her mouth around the bit while she bobs her head and gives the place a curious once over. I don't know exactly what comes over me, but I ask her for a trot. She steps out into a walk, and I ask her again so she bounds into a long, bouncy stride. Kali is a natural at plenty of things, but she wouldn't know a halt to trot transition if it smacked her in the face.

I mindlessly steer her into a figure eight, going for one almost complete circle before starting another one. Kali goes with it, getting the motions down before I ask her to bend. She never stalls, because all she really truly knows is *go, go, go*.

Figure eights become serpentines, which become circles and loops. Kali does it all with interest, learning the motions in our nondescript field. I keep her at a trot, not wanting to overload her head with lead changes. She's a young horse, she's a new horse, and she's a racehorse above all. I don't know what I'm accomplishing with this other than trying to instill a better sense of balance.

We do the last few rounds back at a figure eight at a walk, Kali stepping underneath me with a sense of purpose instead of gearing down lackadaisically and letting me do all the work. She's a good horse. I halt her in the middle of our makeshift workspace and take a look at the tracks we've beaten down in the grass. They crisscross all over the place, indicative that my filly is definitely learning the ropes.

I stop myself right there, before I can do something stupid like form an attachment that will only be broken. I sit on Kali's back and look down at her eye as she turns her head, pricking her ears at something in the distance. It's too easy to get lost in riding Kali, in seeing potential when there probably is none. Kali isn't a winner, and she's hardly even a racer. Everything I'm doing out here is a waste of time, and will only make it harder in the long run when I lose her, because Kali most certainly isn't my filly. She's hardly even Delaney's, seeing as how much he'd like to see her elsewhere.

My chest is tight and I suck in a breath, forcing the air in and out. I tell myself that Kali is learning something from these rides, experiencing something other than speed, so next time she runs maybe there will be a spark.

I loosen my fingers on the reins, leaning forward to pat Kali liberally on the neck.

"Good girl," I tell her, and nudge her forward, keeping it at a walk. We meander back to the barn, not because there's no direct path back, but because I am deliberately taking my time.

∽

By the time we get back from the track, all the lights in the loft are on, because Martina has this irrational need to turn on lights and then forgets to turn them off when she leaves a room. But she's ordered food and has it out on the kitchen table when Dad and I arrive.

I look at her gratefully while Dad digs in, and she shrugs.

"I needed some comfort food," she says by way of explanation. "I figured you two were too busy to think about things like eating."

Okay, maybe I'm less grateful. I don't let that stop me from pulling the cheeseburger she's ordered for me out of the bag and tugging back the paper wrapping. Martina sits down and picks at her French fries, tracing them through ketchup and licking the salt off her fingers. Typical of me, I down the food quickly, like I have somewhere important to be, and think about taking a shower before Martina says something that completely floors me.

"I heard about Blackbridge today," she says, looking at Dad because she knows as well as I do that he's said nothing on the topic. For a second, I'm astonished that she's said anything.

"Who did you talk to?" I ask suddenly, before Dad can speak. Martina shrugs, as if to say that isn't the most important thing.

Martina crumbles up the paper the food came in, getting up and shoving it into the trash. "Something about financial disorder? I heard it was a possible bankruptcy."

"Martina," Dad says, while Martina bangs through the kitchen and stands next to me. They're glaring at each other, like I'm not even involved here. I really don't think this is fair, considering how little Martina is even involved in this supposed business, but I don't know where to begin.

"So what's going on?" Martina demands, when something dawns on me.

"Who told you?" I ask, because there was no way she knew about this last night. That would have been on her list of things to figure out, and maybe she was drunk last night, but you don't forget things so easily when you're drunk. Usually you blurt them out because you don't have the ability to keep it all inside.

"Who doesn't know about it?" Martina shoots back. "Everyone knows. I was at the diner and the cashier asked me how things were going, for Christ's sake."

We both watch Dad wipe his fingers off with an abused, crinkled napkin. He nods, which is a big deal for him. Then he says something that I basically expected, "Mr. Delaney's firm got caught up in some bad investments last month. There's no word yet on what that means for the farm, but I don't want either of you two thinking that things are worse than they are."

He gets up to throw away the greasy paper and napkins, washes his hands while Martina and I look at each other. This is what happens when you've been kept in the dark one too many times. We have to overanalyze everything, wonder what two brief sentences could really mean.

I don't want to leave it at that. "How bad could it be?"

He walks around the kitchen counter, drying his hands with a dish towel that he tosses down on the Formica. "I'll let you know when I know, sweetie."

Martina and I sit quietly, weighing his words.

"I'm going to finish up some work downstairs," he says. "If you need me I'll be in the office."

He escapes, and we don't try to keep him there. The door clicks shut behind him.

"What do you think?" Martina asks, sounding conspiratorial and one step away from jumping up and dragging Dad back up to the loft so we can take turns interrogating him. It's a lovely thought, but it would be pointless. Dad has never been accustomed to sharing emotions, especially not with his daughters. That was always Mom's department, and even then we were secondary to the horses.

I push the papers into the bag they came from and stand up, throwing them away. "I think there's nothing to think."

"What do you mean?" Martina asks, clearly puzzled by my reaction. "He has to know something."

"Maybe it's more complicated than what we're making it," I tell her, suddenly aggravated with everything, not to mention that it's Martina who comes in, blows up, and now I'm left with information I already know. I didn't need this. It needed to be subtler, less confrontational, less involved with making it something it isn't, because this definitely isn't espionage and the last thing I needed was Martina turning it into just that.

"It's as easy as he wants to make it," Martina says. "There has to be something. Even if he doesn't know one hundred percent what's going on, he has an idea. Hell, July, I would go with an opinion. Just something to make me feel better."

I don't want to laugh at that, I really don't. I do anyway.

"You?"

"Yes," Martina says through her teeth. "I'm a part of this family too, July. What happens here doesn't just affect you."

I sober at that. "I would never think that."

"Sure," Martina says, crossing her arms. "Sure you wouldn't, July."

"Of course it doesn't just affect me. But color me shocked that you show up out of the blue and a day later start demanding answers to questions I haven't even been able to formulate yet. The answers you got out of Dad, Martina? I kind of already knew them."

"And you didn't tell me."

"Nope," I say. "I didn't, mainly because you never wanted to talk to me, but also because I don't know if there's anything to know yet. And maybe, Martina, maybe whatever happens is impossible to avoid and we should learn to deal with the unexpected."

"Like you're good at that," Martina says, shaking her long brown hair over her shoulder, the stance she makes that screams confidence and stubbornness rolled into one.

"Maybe not," I concede. "But I think that Dad's answers are temporary ones at best."

Martina narrows her eyes at me. "Who did *you* talk to?"

"Beck."

She pauses, and then nods. "And what did he say?"

"We'll all have to give up something," I say, remembering his words. The reality seems to be that he doesn't know what that really means, but it's pretty obvious. When you own a horse farm for nothing other than the enjoyment of it, it's considered a luxury. You don't give up the essentials when you're stuck in a hard spot. You give up the things you don't need.

"So you were waiting for some confirmation."

"I guess," I say, the fight leaving me. All of a sudden, I'm tired. "Maybe I wanted Dad to say something for once. It didn't have to be answers."

"Then be glad I showed up," Martina says, standing up and walking over to her room. "Unless you really enjoyed all that tiptoeing around the issue."

She shuts her door behind her, hard.

Chapter Twelve

Four days later, I get on Lighter. It's supposed to be his first real gallop since his race. Usually this means it's a laid back romp around the track, but with Lighter it provides him opportunity to get bored and start acting up. I could really use something that will keep his attention, but inevitably nothing except full speed ahead really grasps Lighter.

Martina rides next to me on Maggie, my mare giving the colt a distrustful glare. Lighter is a challenge, and I know Martina's legs are tighter than usual given that she hasn't ridden a horse in a good year or two. The thing about Martina is she was always a technical, beautiful rider. She learned to be good at it, and then she stopped to make a point.

"Are you okay?" I ask her, and she grunts while Lighter continually tosses and moves his head around, like he knows he has a newbie and he has some room to find an advantage. I try to help Martina out, riding Lighter with a quiet insistence that I know he is trying to disregard completely.

"I should ask you that question," Martina says, finally allowing Lighter to do what he wants and place his head in her lap. He looks around her wildly, ears flicking all over the place. Maggie sighs dramatically. "Isn't this the hellion horse?"

"They've all got their moments," I say, mainly because I'm trying not to unnerve Martina.

"July, I'm not an idiot."

"Okay, yes, he's the devil horse. I'm being forced to ride him because I lost a bet with Beck, Dad apparently thinks that's funny, and you showed up, so now you get to help out with him."

Martina makes a face.

"Yeah, well, you asked."

We walk onto the track. Martina lets go of me before I ask, and leaves me to Lighter's devices. He stands perfectly still. I suppose he's considering his options, so I have to give him a command before he takes it into his head to do something I don't like. I spur him into action and he lifts himself into a ground-eating trot. I push him into a canter, and he lowers his head to lean on my hold on the reins.

I let the reins slip through my fingers, and Lighter reacts quickly to keep from falling face first into the dirt. I feel a thrill of victory, but I know it will be short lived when Lighter swerves toward the rail. So it begins.

I gather the reins up again, not planning to make a habit of giving Lighter space, and straighten him out. Lighter recovers quickly and goes faster, breaking into a gallop. We're going along well enough, arguing with each other over how much rein he thinks he deserves, when he shies at nothing and skips to the side, bumping into the rail. The plastic side beam cracks hard against my ankle. A gasp slips through my mouth and I shift my weight without thinking about it. Simultaneously, Lighter switches leads, jumps to the right and shies again, veering so far to the outside of the track he could have blindsided another runner and there's nothing I could have done to stop him.

Racehorses are supposed to run straight, not zigzag across the track like a deranged house cat. I shift him back to the rail, trying not to let this become a complete training disaster. We finish the first lap and I try asking for a canter. Miraculously, Lighter listens. He's shivering, and I roll my eyes.

"I would give you some slack if you could see ghosts, buddy," I tell him, reaching up and running my hand down his mane. Mistake. There's a twitch in his step and he ducks to the inside. I don't have much of a chance to get my weight where it should be, because I'm already flipping over his shoulder and landing on my back on the dirt.

The sky is so, so blue.

I want to strangle that colt. I wait to hear him dash off, but instead there's a warm, slightly slobbery muzzle that pushes into my face. Lighter has taken it upon himself to check me out, nudging my crash helmet, then my neck and then snuffling around my hips like he's sure I must be down here for a reason other than he is a big jerk of a horse.

"I don't have treats," I tell him, and Lighter lifts his head like I've just insulted him.

"Hey, Juls?" I hear Beck, and right now I do want to hit him. A jab to his shoulder would make me feel better.

"This is your fault, you know," I say as he offers me his hand.

"Well, you made a bad bet," he says right back, unaffected. "Think you can stand?"

"I can try," I say, taking his hand and letting him lift me up to my feet. My whole back seizes, and I must have wavered, because he puts one hand on my hip and lifts the other to my face, tipping my head up to look me over appraisingly.

"You didn't hit your head, did you?"

"I thumped the back of it pretty good," I say, and he scowls at that, putting his thumb under my chin so he can turn my head back and forth, like mobility has something to do with how bruised my brain is right now.

"I'm okay," I say, a hot flush seeping over my skin while he still holds onto me. It's nothing, I tell myself. He's just a boy, and boys look concerned sometimes. Sometimes they hold on to you too long. It's nothing at all. I shake out of his grip and his hands fall back to his sides.

"Just making sure," he says, turning his scowl to his horse. "Little bastard."

"Sure," I laugh, too high-pitched and pained. My legs are shaky, but they hold me up well enough. "Now you agree with me."

"Well, it was a pretty inspired move on his part."

"So says you," I say, making my way over to Lighter, who is still standing there like this conversation fascinates him.

"Juls," Dad yells at me from across the track. "If you can, give him another lap at a jog. I think that first one was too fast, so you can relax the second one."

I want to say I cannot believe this, but I turn from Dad to Beck and say, "Give me a leg up?"

He doesn't even look surprised. Instead he nods to the horse. "Let's go."

I gather up Lighter's reins, lift a leg into Beck's hands, and jump. He lifts me the rest of the way until I get a leg over Lighter's back and settle into the saddle. Beck squeezes my knee and pushes off of me. Lighter takes a few prancing steps to the side as I collect myself and wish I could brush the feeling of Beck's hands off my body.

"Remember, Juls," he says as I begin to walk away. "Today's word is relaxation."

I manage a carefree laugh. "Shut up," I say over my shoulder, and then ask Lighter to pick up the pace.

~~

I'm hurting already when we file into the grandstand to watch Diver run in the Sword Dancer Invitational. My whole back aches, from my shoulders down to my thighs. My right arm landed awkwardly on the ground, and I'm lucky I didn't break it. My left ankle hates life in general. In fact, I notice a bit of a limp.

"Need me to carry you?" Beck asks when he notices I don't exactly have a spring in my step.

"As pathetic as it might sound," I say, easing myself down the short flight of stairs to our box, "I might take you up on that."

He stops a step below me and turns, blocking any way I can advance down the stairs.

"Beck," I say, pushing at his chest to let me pass.

"You asked," he reminds me, and lifts me so unexpectedly I almost scream. And then I have to bite back a cry as my back muscles twinge in protest. I can't tell if this is conven- ient or simply awful. Then there's the part of me, nearly drowned out by the sheer pain, that is recording in stunning detail every second of this because Beck is being sweet and I am letting him. This part of me is simply overjoyed. I think it's the part of me that might like the occasional romance novel, actually.

I crush this feeling as Beck shifts me in his arms and a bolt of pain laces through my abused muscles.

"Okay?" he asks, oblivious to my dueling reactions. I nod.

"Let's just get there, please?"

He does as asked, depositing me in the box and getting a button on his suit jacket caught in the hem of my dress. He frees himself and slips behind me. I notice Martina giving me a half-smile, and I don't have the energy to tell her to keep her comments to herself. She's not really commenting, so I know I'll only get a plea of her innocence. Of course she is not thinking suspicious thoughts. Right.

Diver stumbles at the start, but in a mile and a half race he's got some time to make up for it. He falls into line in last, not too far behind the rest of the field. Jorge keeps him where he is, saving ground and energy trying to get Diver to a position the gelding more commonly chooses for himself. Diver isn't a late closer, but today he will be.

It doesn't suit him. Already I can see him climbing, lifting his front legs too high, like he's trying to jump the clods of turf that are raining back from the hooves of the horses in front of him. He's weaving, like he wants to run, but Jorge keeps holding him back.

When he finally gets to go, he practically explodes. He throws everything he has into it, racing down the middle of the track and finishing a driving third. Pretty good for the few miserable opportunities he had.

The prospect of walking down to the paddock and back up is too daunting, especially since there's only one more race of the day, a maiden special weight that Kali could have run in if Delaney didn't want to get rid of her. Instead we have another horse in it, a three-year-old colt that may or may not make something of himself eventually. Either way, I can't make myself go down to the paddock to watch him, so I sit down in my chair and watch everyone else head down to the paddock.

Beck squeezes my aching shoulder before he leaves, and it actually feels good.

"Good choice, kiddo," he says, leaning down over my shoulder.

"Please stop calling me that," I sigh, and he chuckles, leaving the box.

Martina plops down next to me, smoothing out her skirt and crossing her legs. I look at her warily. Martina always thinks there is a hopeless romantic somewhere inside of me, clawing desperately to get out. It's the fact that I've never had a boyfriend, never been kissed, that drives her to this conclusion. So when she sees an opportunity, she never fails to point it out to me. I try to avoid these moments, and this time my body isn't in any shape to flee.

"So," she says, innocently enough.

I already can't stand it. "Okay, stop."

"I wasn't saying anything!"

"You were going to say something so awful I might've had to leave, despite all of my protesting muscles."

"Now you're being dramatic," Martina says, leaning back in her seat. "It's not my fault that I have to be observant."

"Oh my God."

"You really need to go forth and have fun, Juls."

"Excuse me?"

"Stop acting so dense, July," Martina demands. "You can open your eyes at any time."

"You're so absurdly romantic," I say to her.

"And you're nearly eighteen," she informs me, like I don't know this. "Not dead."

She nudges my shoulder and gets up to follow everyone else.

~⁓

Dad refuses to let me do much work after the races, and I'm grateful because all I really want to do is take over the bathroom and soak in the tub. I fill the basin with scalding hot water, and sink into it, watching my skin flush pink. My muscles unwind, and the pain in my bruising ankle trickles away. It will be back full force tomorrow, but right now is a reprieve, and I've already cracked open the bottle of Ibuprofen to help make it bearable.

I sink further into the water, letting it wash up over my shoulders and my neck. It feels good enough to sleep in, but I restrain that impulse. I would much rather appreciate this first hand. Maybe I'd like to catalog what the aches and pains are, and how they all slip away momentarily, so I can complain to Beck about it tomorrow when they'll be raging and awful.

Since Martina agreed to ride Maggie when I'm relegated to the racers, Beck has casually bowed out of works, preferring to be ringside audience rather than active member of the circus going on inside the training oval. I don't blame him, but for whatever reason there's a stab of disappointment every morning he elects to not jump up in the saddle.

I'm drying off and pulling on a fresh pair of jeans when I hear the commotion start.

"I know it's too late to start classes this semester," Martina rages, incensed. I stay in the bathroom, not wanting to intervene, like a sane person. "I didn't exactly plan all of this through yet, Dad. It just happened."

"You've been stalling for the better part of three years," Dad says. "We both know you weren't making any plans at all. Not with that kid. What's his name."

"Scott," Martina grinds out, and I recognize that voice. That's her stay-out-of-it voice, the one she's used a lot with me, especially when we were kids.

"You can't keep running from any sort of responsibility, Martina."

"I'm not doing that."

There's a pregnant pause. I pull my shirt on and push my damp hair back from my face, the last of the water pooling down the drain suddenly very loud in the room.

"You want me to make a plan?" Martina asks. "Fine. I am planning on not getting married at twenty-one and having a couple of unplanned kids, and then getting hastily and unnecessarily divorced."

I wince at that one, because that's a low blow. Dad surprises me when he says, "I'm glad to hear that, Martina. I want to know what else you've got in store for yourself."

The lack of an answer means that Martina is surprised too. The resulting slammed door means that she doesn't have an answer at all. Everything goes very silent. I hear the front door open and shut, so now I'm alone. Martina won't emerge from her room until she knows everyone in the loft is gone, so I decide to help her out.

I towel dry my hair, rip a brush through it, and slip out of the bathroom. I toe on my flip-flops and leave as quietly as possible. The light is on in Dad's office, and I head out of the barn the other way, not knowing where I'm going other than

I know I want to get out of the barn. Right when I get to the parking lot, I realize I've left my car keys in the loft, and I don't really want to go back, so I walk.

It's humid and warm out. I can see the breeding barns across the main road, their lights glowing in the dark. Above me, in the clouds I can't see because night seems to have come so quickly, thunder rolls.

I hear the rain before it gets to me, and then I'm standing in a torrential downpour. That's just great. I'm too far away from the barn to turn back and make a run for it, but I am pretty close to the main house. I hesitate about that, right there in the rain, and when a lightning bolt streaks down and darts off to touch the ground on the opposite side of the training oval, I book it out of there.

The main house has its lights on, and Beck's red Mustang sits in the open garage. I run up the stairs and hunker under the portico, ringing the doorbell a couple of times because I'm soaked and would really like a place to wait out the storm. A ride back to the barn wouldn't be a bad option either. I chew on my bottom lip, pondering which request I should go with first. I haven't decided by the time Beck opens the door.

The first thing he does is grin. The first thing I do is scowl at him.

"You know," he says, "I was wondering what I should do on this fabulous Saturday night, but then you came along and made it such a simple decision."

I push a clump of very wet hair out of my face and try to look dignified. It's not like it really matters in the long run, considering I'm in the presence of a boy who is wearing a T-shirt with a dinosaur riding a tricycle screen printed on it. I think that says a lot.

"Can I please come in, or do you like watching me drip all over your doormat?"

"I guess I can watch you drip all over the floor, too," he shrugs, pushing back from the doorframe and letting me inside. "That's just as fun."

The air conditioning is almost brutal, and what was fairly warm rainwater clinging to my skin turns frigid cold. I feel like I've been dunked in ice water.

"Olivia has some clothes stashed upstairs," Beck says, motioning for me to follow him. "Let's see what she's got."

I walk up the stairs, shivering and incomparably happy when Beck pauses to find a towel in one of the upstairs bathrooms, pushing it into my hands before walking across the hallway and into what can only be Olivia's room.

I stand in the doorway, watching Beck rummage through his sister's things. The fluffy towel has turned damp as I work it through my hair, which isn't a complete loss considering how wet it was before the storm. The rest of me will need a complete going over, as soon as I get a change of clothes.

"Here," Beck finally says, lifting a black T-shirt and an old pair of jeans out of one of Olivia's dressers. I take the clothes that Beck offers, and lock myself into the bathroom, tugging the wet jeans off my clammy legs and drying off. I shimmy into Olivia's clothes, thrilled that they fit.

Beck is leaning against the wall outside the bathroom when I emerge, still feeling damp, but mostly better.

"Good?" he asks.

"Good."

He extends his hand. "Give me the others. We can toss them in the dryer and wait them out."

"Oh," I say, brilliantly, and give him my clothes without thinking while following him again down to the basement. He throws them into the dryer, deciding to bake them for a good hour. I don't argue, but I didn't think I was staying here either. Then again, I hadn't planned to head back to the loft so soon, not with Dad and Martina squaring off every few hours.

"Okay," he says, rubbing his hands together. I really hope that doesn't mean he has some crazy plans, because I am not up for crazy plans right now. "I was going to make something chocolaty. Want to help?"

Call me amazed.

"You're baking?"

"I was planning on baking, yes."

"I don't think I believe you."

He laughs and grabs my hand, tugging me toward the basement steps.

"What are you planning to make?" I ask, walking after him into the kitchen, which would probably make plenty of chefs miserably jealous. I see a bag of chocolate chips on the granite countertop, as well as an assortment of ingredients that don't exactly add up to chocolate chip cookies. I pick up a gallon of milk, bewildered, before putting it back in the fridge.

"I think I have everything," he says, looking around like what is here ought to work somehow.

"I didn't come over here to bake you cookies," I say, because there's no way I'm allowing myself to get talked into baking.

"But you're here, and you know how to do this sort of thing."

Classic Beck whine. I roll my eyes and motion him over. "I will supervise."

While he stares at the chocolate bag, I can feel an explanation of what a tablespoon and a teaspoon are coming on strong, but I pin down that impulse.

"Do what it says on the bag."

To my surprise, he figures it out without my help. So I get to sit on the counter and watch the process, stunned that I'm not the one working. The last time this happened I was eleven years old, wanting desperately to help my mom as I watched her bake all the treats she always refused to eat.

Beck gives me a sideways glance and a smile, as if he knows how much I enjoy this. I try not to let on, but I'm kicking my bare feet, tapping my heels against the cabinets underneath me and hooking my toes on the doorknobs. I must look like an excited little kid.

"So, what are you doing in the middle of a storm?" he finally asks, stirring the whole bag of chips into the mixture.

"Well, the whole point wasn't to get stuck in the storm," I say. "I didn't know it was going to rain when I decided to take a walk."

"Ms. Oblivious," he says, and I shrug. Guilty as charged.

"Admittedly," I say, "I took a walk to get out of the loft."

"Martina?"

"Martina." I nod, focusing my attention on the floor. "That place isn't big enough for all of us."

"You know," he says, pulling a couple of cookie sheets out from the cabinet underneath me. He puts them next to my thigh and squeezes my knee, making me squeak and pull out of his grip. "You're always welcome over here when the family is too much."

"Sure. That would go over great with Dad."

"What, no sleepovers?" he asks, and I smack his arm.

"For that," he says, "you're helping me out with the next part."

"Fine," I slip down to the floor and walk over to the utensil drawer to pull out two spoons. I give him one and dig into the dough. The first thing Beck does is spoon some batter into his mouth.

"That is disgusting," I tell him, grabbing his spoon and giving him a new one.

"Are you telling me you don't like cookie batter?"

"It's uncooked," I say, remembering what Mom always said. "There are eggs in it. It's an easy way to get sick."

He rolls his eyes. "Never mind, I rescind my invitation. Someone who doesn't enjoy chocolate chip cookie dough is way too serious to be in my space for more than an hour, tops."

"Too bad I've kind of been in and out of your space for many years," I say, pleased that he's finally spooning batter onto the cookie sheet.

He smirks. "Not close enough, July."

I pause, narrowing my eyes. "And yet I don't eat uncooked batter, so I guess there's no hope."

He nods sagely. "Batter eaters and non-batter eaters really can't coexist. Your wisdom knows no bounds."

"Thank you," I say, semi-seriously, finishing up my cookie sheet and walking around him to the oven. I pop my sheet in and turn around, stopping short when he's right there in front of me, a blob of uncooked cookie batter wrapped on the tip of his index finger.

"Although," he says, holding his finger in front of me like it's supposed to be tantalizing. Or maybe I can't ignore it, and he knows. "I have a feeling if you try it, you'll never go back to that old lady attitude of yours."

"It's a sensible attitude," I defend myself. He smiles.

"Come on, July. I dare you."

An idea crosses my mind, and I smile. It might be a bit of an evil smile. Beck looks too intrigued, especially when I say, "I think I can make you regret this."

"You'll never know unless you try," he says. It's an open invitation, because he's curious and we both know what this is going to involve. It's not like I'm going to slip around him and bypass the obvious choice. Something in me won't allow that, and a very distinct thrill courses out through my limbs.

I take his hand in mine and lean forward, licking his finger into my mouth. There has to be a trick to this, something about doing the last thing he'll expect, but I don't know if I'm that much of a flirt. The way he's looking down at his hand makes me think it doesn't matter. There's a kind of shock on his face, quickly replaced by an intensity that makes me feel way too warm.

I clean the batter off his finger and pop his finger out of my mouth, chewing thoughtfully on the sugary dough. I drop his hand.

"Sorry to say," I smile at him, licking my lips. "But I still prefer it cooked."

I walk around the island, ignoring the way he's staring after me, because that's giving me a bit of a thrill also.

"I had no idea you could play that dirty," he finally says while I work on his cookie sheet, finishing it and pushing it into the oven. Now we have down time. I might not have planned this well.

"Maybe you don't know me that well," I say, and he shakes his head.

"Oh, no, July. I know you really damn well. Tightly wound neatnik—"

"Neatnik?"

"It's an awesome word," he says.

I smile, picking up the bowl of batter and sticking it in the fridge.

Beck goes on, counting down everything about me. "Horse lover, rule follower, sensible, responsible July. Yet you're bizarrely impulsive."

"That doesn't say a lot about me," I say. "There's more."

"Oh, I know."

I open my mouth and shut it again. He walks around the island and leans a hip against the granite, crossing his arms and giving me that look that dares me to ask him a question he can't answer. Fine. I have one for him.

"You know why my parents named me July?" He can't possibly know that.

"Hell if I know," he says. "You were born in September. Knowing your dad, I'm going to guess that it was a completely random choice."

"You have so failed," I say, victorious.

"I think I should get points for remembering your birth month."

"Like a half point, if that."

"It's something. So why am I named Beckett?"

I don't know. So I take a wild stab at it. "It's your mom's maiden name?"

He laughs, because either I am really wrong or I am right.

"That one wasn't really that hard," he tells me, right when the oven timer dings.

We make batch after batch of cookies, and I keep slapping him away from them while they cool on the paper towels I have spread out on the countertops. By the last batch, it's finally stopped raining, and we pile a ton of the cookies on a paper plate and go outside to sit under the covered porch. There's a line of Adirondack chairs out there, and we sit in the middle, the cookies situated between us. They're still warm, and the first one I put in my mouth melts on my tongue.

"Okay, that was worth it," Beck says, practically inhaling the first cookie he touches and going for a second. The whole batch will be gone in a matter of a day, at the very least.

"You ate that too fast to even taste it," I find myself complaining. "And was being forced to make them by yourself that bad?"

"July," he says, "I could have burned the house down, so sensibly speaking it was definitely a trial. You're lucky you're alive."

"Uh-huh."

We sit for a minute and savor the product of Beck's labor and my supervision in silence, listening as the storm wrings out the last drops of rain. Water drips from the eves and splatters on the floor of the porch. I can almost see the stars as the clouds break up. It's been a good night, I realize somewhat suddenly. It was the very last thing I could have expected, but it was nice all the same.

"So why were you named July?" Beck asks, licking chocolate off of his thumb.

I pause, bringing my knees to my chest and hugging my shins tight. Might as well, right?

"July is my mom's favorite month," I say, resting my cheek against my knees and looking over at him. "She used to always say everything was better in July because that's when Saratoga opens. She always wanted to win a race on opening day."

Beck considers me a moment and says, "Did she ever? Win?"

"No," I say through a slow smile, wondering if that ever bugged her. "She never did. And she hasn't been back in so long she may never."

"That sucks, you know." Beck shakes his head, and I raise an eyebrow. "Not the story," he amends. "That she never comes back."

I shrug, feeling for once the truth of the matter—Mom is miles and miles away, and I'm tired of thinking about the distance. With everything happening here, I want to focus on what's in front of me for once. Mom only muddles my thoughts, and right now I want my head clear.

"It does suck," I acknowledge. "I think about her too much."

"Yeah," Beck says through a short laugh. "How can you not? If my mom did that I'd be more of a wreck than I already am. Or I'd be headed to Wall Street, like Matt." He makes a show of shivering.

"Stop," I laugh. "You're not a wreck. You're . . . you."

"Is that a compliment?" he asks, giving me a disbelieving look.

"Maybe," I hedge. "If agreeing you are not a wreck is a compliment, then I'll allow it."

"I think that's the sweetest thing you've ever said to me," he says, pressing his hand to his heart.

"Don't get used to it," I tell him.

"Believe me, I won't," he counters, and then looks down at his hands in what I can only describe is a rare moment of introspection. Then, "Your mom doesn't deserve it, you know."

"What?" I ask, meeting his eyes when he looks up at me. He smiles ruefully, just a lift in the corner of his mouth.

"Any of your time."

A shy blush blossoms across my cheeks and I duck my head. "I'll keep that under consideration."

"Good to hear," he says, reaching for another cookie.

By the time the cookies are gone I realize it's late and I need to find my sandals. It's wet out, but I can still walk in it. I remember my clothes are probably sitting wrinkled in the dryer, so I go down to collect them, shimmying into them right there. I walk up the basement steps and put Olivia's folded clothes on the kitchen counter.

"Thanks," I tell Beck. He consumes the last bit of cookie between his fingers.

"Thanks for helping," he says. "Maybe next time you can bake them for me."

"I really don't think that's going to happen."

He nods, walking me to the door. "Yeah, but a guy can dream."

I shake my head at that, backing out of the door and onto the drying front steps of the house. It's humid as hell out, and my hair has dried into all sorts of chaotic waves. Beck leans his shoulder against the doorframe and looks bright, mischievous. It's in his eyes, in his body. I can see that he's having trouble standing still, while managing to appear like he's perfectly content where he is.

"See you at dawn?" I ask.

"That's the plan."

I nod and turn around, heading out over the slick grass on a shortcut to the barn. The lights are off in the loft, so I have definitely realized my goal of avoiding everyone for the night. I'm feeling pretty good until I hear Beck call my name and I come to a slippery stop on the dew-drenched lawn. I turn, not expecting to find Beck walking up to me. He's barefoot and the door to the house is gaping open, light spilling out onto the front steps.

I expect to see bright and happy Beck running up to me with something I forgot, but I forgot nothing and the smile has fled his face. I can't even pinpoint how he looks, because before I can start thinking of adjectives he's right there and his hands are in my humidity thick hair and he catches my mouth with his.

It's a quick kiss that sends my heart on a chaotic race in my chest. He backs up a scant few inches, looking into my eyes. Instinctively, I lift my hands to his wrists, wrap my fingers around them, and am further shocked when he comes back to kiss me again, harder, more sure of this whole insane thing that we're doing. Warmth radiates its way up to my skin, and every pulse point in my body thrums along to my galloping heartbeat.

Then he releases me, my hands falling from his skin. He's bright again, green flashing in his eyes when his mouth quirks into that smile.

"Just getting you back, July."

I could hit him, but before I can he's backing up, that ever-present laugh on his lips, and turns to jog back to his house. I whip around, tell myself not to think—do not even *think*—and march home.

Chapter Thirteen

Not thinking about it doesn't work. I can't not think about it. Every time I find myself spacing out, there he is, stupid Beck, with this stupid smile on his stupid lips. I want to bang my head against something solid and be done with it, but I can't do that. It wouldn't help.

That night, I can't help staying awake, stuck there in bed with the sheets wrapped around my legs and twisted around my waist. I'm aching everywhere, but it's in the back of my mind, almost forgotten, because instead I run that kiss through my head, an endless loop that I can obsess over in a way that would definitely make Beck laugh.

I guess this isn't exactly unexpected. How is a girl supposed to react to her first kiss? A stolen first kiss, I might add? A stolen first kiss with a person who did it *to get back at me*? To get back at me for a bet that *I lost*? I don't think I deserved that, and I know Beck is somewhere smirking his fool head off. Jackass.

A week goes by, but I'm not quite sure I even notice.

All of this dwelling makes morning works challenging. I don't know exactly where my head is at any given moment, and this makes riding Lighter like having a death wish. I have to get my head back in order, or I'm sunk, especially with the Travers speeding around the corner.

I sit on Maggie, keeping light contact with her mouth while we both watch the works in relative silence. Over by the raised clocking stand, Dad is standing with a stopwatch. Beck is next to him. I know this because I've ridden past them enough times, glaring straight forward while I try to make a subtle point that I'm not going to look at Beck. I figure looking is telling, and I don't want to tell Beck anything.

I don't know what I want to do with Beck. I think that's my main problem.

"Do you realize I've been yelling at you for a solid minute?" Martina asks, pulling up next to me on one of our other ponies, a solid buckskin gelding named Rudy. I start and stare at her, not knowing what to say.

"I'm sorry?"

Martina rolls her eyes. "Whatever. I was telling you that I'm taking Rudy back to the barn. Dad wants you to pick up Star when he's done with the breeze, and call it a day. When is Bri getting in?"

"After the races," I tell her. Bri is spending a long weekend with us at the farm. We've already gotten to that point, and I wonder where the month went.

Martina watches Star for a minute, the dark colt flying through a blow out before his race. She doesn't really seem to absorb it. Mostly it's just a horse that is running, and sometimes I get that. I see it enough as it is, but Star is something else. He's perfectly balanced, quick on his feet, so responsive that it easily makes him more than just a running horse. He's going to be the next Travers winner. At his rate, he's at the top of his game, right up there with Hot Metal. It will be a fun race to witness.

"I'm not going to the races today," Martina says as Star flashes past the last marker and begins to gallop out. He'll be on us within a minute.

"What?" I ask, not sure I understand her. "Why?"

"We've got, what, one horse running in an optional claimer?" Martina asks. "I don't need to be there for that. I'll stay back and fix up the loft while you're helping Dad. You've been so out of it lately, I figure you need the help."

Martina taps Rudy's sides and they trot off before I can say anything. Star comes cruising around the turn. I reach for him right when I choose to look up, catching Beck watching me. Beck being who he is, doesn't bother to look away. In fact, he waves.

I nearly fall off my horse.

"Hey," Jorge says, reaching out to grab my hand when I miss Star's bridle and nearly snag the reins. "You okay?"

"Fine," I lie. My cheeks are flaming, and I duck my head down to hide the flush. I slip the line into the right spot, and we ride back to the barn. I make it a point not to look back.

～

"July!" Bri yells at me as she drives into the parking lot, waving at me from her open window. I'm in the doorway of the barn, pointing her to where to park, when Beck walks up behind me.

"Who's that?"

To my horror, my heart leaps to a gallop. He's right at my back, a warm presence standing too close.

"That's Bri."

"The girl I don't know?"

I turn, and am presented with another one of his insane shirts, this time depicting a whale and a squid in an epic battle to the death, and decide that ignoring him is fruitless. He's watching Bri perfect her parking job with increasing bemusement.

"That's the one," I say, walking into the sunny parking lot.

"Hey," I say, stopping at Bri's car and looking into the trunk, where she's got two large suitcases that I'm sure she didn't need to bring for a long weekend. Bri overpacks like nobody's business.

"Hi," Bri says, then shades her hand over her eyes to look up at the barn, where Beck continues to stand, like a sentry. He waves at her, and I give him a look that seems to brighten his day because he plants himself against the side of the door and watches with interest.

"Who is that?" Bri asks, and I sigh.

"That's Beck."

"Really?" Bri asks, laughing.

"Yeah," I agree, my mind traitorously zooming right back to that damned kiss. I shake it loose, tell myself to forget about it once and for all, because it's been over a week since that kiss and nothing at all has come of it. For all I know, it's his sick way of amusing himself when he's bored.

That's when my head reminds me that he tasted like chocolate. I'd like to kick the crap out of my brain.

"Are you okay?" Bri asks, reaching out and touching my arm.

"Sure," I shrug, shaking those stupid thoughts out and wishing it would be easy to sweep them right out of my subconscious. "Why do you ask?"

"You're blushing like crazy," Bri says, looking at me with concern.

"It's nothing," I say, waving it off. "It's hot."

"Okay," Bri shrugs. "So I didn't get anything to eat. Is there a place we can go?"

"Sure there is," Beck says, having walked up from the barn, because he can't help himself. He offers Bri his hand, and she takes it.

"I'm Beck."

"Bri," she says. "July's friend."

Bri sneaks a smile at me and, of course, this doesn't go unnoticed by Beck. He grins, like he can tell what's going through Bri's head, and I restrict the impulse to smack his arm. He only smiles wider.

Kill me now.

We go to Rustic, and all through dinner I know Beck is winning over Bri to the extent that would be truly frightening if I wasn't used to it. He turns on the charm to the point of absurdity, sweeping Bri up in a roller coaster of charisma that I know she can't possibly resist. Even I can't help smiling at the way she hangs on his every word, and I'm probably failing miserably at hiding it.

"Wow," is all Bri says when he jumps up to go to the bar to pay our bill. She's blatantly staring at him. I follow her eyes to Beck's back and then turn quickly to Bri, who now finally has a turn to blush.

"Don't judge me," Bri demands, and I raise my hands.

"I wasn't," I say. "That's sort of how he is."

"I don't know how you keep up with him," Bri laughs, leaning back in her booth and picking up her glass of soda, drinking the last bit of it.

"No one ever said I did," I say, just as Beck returns, shoving his wallet into the back pocket of his jeans.

"Never did what?" he asks, putting one hand on the back of the booth and leaning toward me.

"Keep up with you," I say easily, and he blinks.

"Well," he says, shifting his weight to the side to allow me space to get out of the booth. Bri follows along, digging in her purse as a ruse to make us think she's not paying strict attention. "I think our game is more tit for tat, don't you think?"

I smile up at him. "That remains to be seen."

Because he is entirely right, he says, "Ball's in your court, Juls."

"I think that's a horrible idea."

He scoffs. "I think you're capable."

At this point, Bri has given up searching through her bag for a nonexistent item. She stares at us, and I pull my keys from my bag. I think this is my cue to drive us all home, before anyone gets any ideas and I'm left with some awkward notions to dispel. Awkward notions that may or may not be true, but it still doesn't mean I want to deal with them.

"Alright, kids," I say, slapping Beck hard enough in the stomach to at least get him to stop giving me that smart aleck grin. He sighs.

"Always the violence, July."

"Always the smart ass, Beckett."

"You like it," he says with enough confidence to make my stomach flip. Bri's head turns again, watching me like a hawk. I usher everyone out, quickly.

Quark Star stands like a pro in front of the cameras on Saturday afternoon, his polished coat glowing a blue black. Not a hair is out of place, mainly because I helped Izzie give him two baths before we trailered him over. You could eat off this horse's coat, he's so perfectly manicured.

Bri stays well away from the horses, watching with interest but unwilling to approach. Beck stands with her, despite the crush of people standing in the saddling paddock, his group of friends gathered nearby, and his parents in attendance for the Travers, or what's affectionately called the Summer Derby. On my end of things, it's a melee. From Bri's perspective, it must be claustrophobic, standing in a maxed out yard with nine half-ton animals circling around the perimeter.

I dart across the walkway, stepping into the well-trodden grass. Star walks by, his head down by Gus's wrist and his whole body coiled behind him. His neck is arched and he's picking up his feet in the exaggerated manner of an excited circus horse. Behind him Hot Metal is a coppery chestnut firestorm. Bri gives the Derby winner one awed glance and sinks back behind Beck's shoulder.

"Who is that?" she asks, while Beck is too amused that he has a girl cowering behind him.

"That's Hot Metal," I tell her. "He's not on his best behavior today."

The moment I say that, the colt rears, completely petulant. Then he drops back to all fours and is allowed to stand for a minute, before being urged on. He goes, looks more put together by some miracle, but he's swishing his tail too much, like a cat waiting to attack.

Quark Star, on the other hand, is fairly content, if nervous. This is a packed house, and Star isn't as well adjusted to the sheer numbers as a Derby winner.

"At least he's the only one," Bri says, canvassing the other entries from behind Beck, finally stepping around him when Hot Metal has thrashed past us. "That brown one over there looks half-asleep. I think we'd get along."

Beck chuckles at that while he thumbs through the day's program. "Lucrative."

"What?" Bri asks

"That's his name," Beck supplies. "Not a bad choice. You betting?"

Bri laughs. "I don't see the point."

"Come on," Beck says. "You're not really at the races if you don't have two bucks on a horse."

"He doesn't mean that," I tell her, and Bri looks between us, trying to decide who she should believe.

"I don't think you know my betting practices, July," he tells me, and I really don't believe we're having this conversation, but I can't make myself stop.

"It's not like I always see you at the windows, Beck."

"Okay, wait," Bri breaks in. "Can someone at least show me? I'll do it."

"I will," I say, leading the way out of the paddock with Bri on my heels.

"You two," Bri says as I pick out the least insane line at the closest bank of windows, "are definitely at something."

"Beck is usually at something," I tell her, pushing away a stray section of hair that has worked its way free from the bobby pins Martina tortured me with earlier.

"No, no," Bri says, trying to clarify. "I mean, I'm used to seeing you steadfastly avoid guys you like, as if that's a productive or even sane thing to do, so I wasn't really sure at first, but you like him."

"I hate to say this, Bri," I shake my head. "You are very wrong."

She has me. We both know it, just by the way she's giving me her pleased to death look. That blush creeps back up my neck. "You *like* like him," Bri says in a singsong voice. "Plus, you look like a cooked lobster."

"It's hot," I say defensively. "And it's sunny."

"And you like Beck," Bri adds, watching me through narrowed eyes. "Can I please have details now?"

"There are no details."

Bri works her jaw back and forth, considering me. "You're lying."

"Would you stop doing that?"

"July."

"Bri."

She is impossible sometimes. So, so impossible.

"It's stupid," I tell her, and she lights up like a firecracker.

"Tell me everything," she begs, practically dancing on her toes. "Please tell me everything."

"It was like a week ago," I tell her, intending to give her a short overview that devolves rapidly into the long version. I totally give in and crack. "And it was to get back at me because I licked cookie dough off his stupid finger, or maybe because I lost a bet. I don't know what's happening anymore. He's stupid, and it's stupid, and I'm stupid. Okay?"

"No!" Bri exclaims, shaking her head. "July, it's not stupid. It's a game."

"It's an idiotic game."

"Well, yeah," Bri shrugs. "I guess they usually are. But you have to do something now. You haven't done anything, have you?"

"I really need to tell you at least something about betting before we get to the window," I say, trying to turn this conversation around. I don't really want to tell her that I've done nothing except stare into space for the past week, because that isn't me. That isn't what I want to be, and I definitely don't want to wait around to see what happens. But therein is my problem. I'm not exactly sure what I want to do, even with Beck practically challenging me to my face at Rustic.

Ball's in my court? Well, what the hell do I do with it? Why do I have it to begin with?

"I know you hate it when I talk about initiative," Bri says, totally ignoring me, "but I think this is a perfect time for this talk."

"Okay," I say, "A win bet is pretty self-explanatory . . ."

"I know you're really good at pining, July," she says, talking over me. "Like, epically good at it. I think you're too comfortable with it, if you want to know the truth. I mean, look at that Diver thing, right? Your mom? Do you see where I'm going with this?"

"That's great," I say. "Compare my situation with Beck to my inability to buy a horse and my wayward mother. That makes loads of sense."

"You are so negative," Bri says with a sigh.

"So, anyway," I start over again, "it's self-explanatory. If you bet the horse to win it has to obviously win. If you bet to place the horse has to win or come in second, but the return is less. If . . ."

"And I know you," Bri launches back into it. "You could let this go because you'd rather pine and watch everything slip away than actually do something."

"But Beck isn't slipping away," I argue, her comment striking a nerve. I don't let things go, and definitely not on purpose. "He won't even leave."

"Exactly!" Bri says excitedly. "He isn't. God, July, it's set up so perfectly. You don't even have to wonder about him."

"Of course I have to wonder about him," I say. "He's Beck. Did I not complain about him enough before?"

"This also isn't the rest of your life, you know," Bri points out. "You need to be a teenager for, like, half a second. I think you need at least one shot at a boyfriend before you enter college. A summer fling, at the very least, and we're running out of summer."

"You might want to do across the board on Lucrative, because it will pay out three ways if he wins."

"I'm not betting on Lucrative," Bri says, marching up to the window when it's our turn and plunking down her two dollars.

"Quark Star," she says. "To win."

∿

When we get back to the saddling paddock, the horses are on their way out. Quark Star ambles by, with Jorge grinning at us from the saddle. The crowd has thinned considerably, most people hunting for good spots to view the race if they don't have seats in the stands. Delaney and his family are taking their time with Dad and Martina. Beck is still standing in the grass of the saddling paddock, talking with his friends.

The blond girl has one thin arm laced around his. Beck's hands are pocketed in his trousers, his weight back on his heels. It's almost sad how little attention he's giving back to the girl pressed against his side.

"See?" I tell Bri, and she pokes me sharply with her elbow.

"Do you even know who they are?"

It's embarrassing to admit that I don't know them at all, so I let my silence speak for me.

"You don't know them, do you?" It's a question, but it doesn't sound like it.

"No," I say. "They're probably college friends. They're new this year."

She sighs at me.

"In my defense, it's not like he's introduced them to me."

That gets me absolutely nowhere with Bri, who takes that as the excuse it is and doesn't bother to respond. We wait for the last of the horses to parade out to the track, and then cross over to our group before heading up into the stands.

Quark Star prances right into the gate, his ears far forward. He's in the third stall, given time to settle in or get wound up. Horses are loaded alongside him, one after the other until Hot Metal stands in abject terror at the gates in front of him. He takes one look and digs in his heels.

"What's happening?" Bri asks as Martina sighs next to me, shifting her weight while the starters begin the tedious process.

"They'll try to force him in," I tell her, watching Hot Metal kick his hind legs, the jockey coming off intentionally. It's better to jump down than get thrown, but it's a sign no one likes to see. In the gate, I can see Quark Star's head turned sideways, noticing the drama.

Sometimes it's a hiccup when a horse doesn't want to go into the gate, and other times there's a good reason. Hot Metal never acts like this on any good day, but so far he's been having about as off a day as he can get. The starters throw the blindfold over his eyes and lead him in two tight circles, then right into the gate. As soon as the starters move to close the gate, he goes completely bonkers.

I hear the thuds of muscle against metal in the stands, and it takes a very dedicated assistant starter to hold on to the colt's head as he flies backward out of the gate, bucking and thrashing. Murmurs ripple through the crowd as Hot Metal calms down enough to be led far behind the gate, where a vet stands waiting to take a look at him.

Meanwhile, all the other horses have to be backed out and reloaded. I lean against the railing and get comfortable, watching the proceedings with as much single-minded attention as everyone else. If Hot Metal has one cut on him—just one—he'll be scratched from the race. As the favorite, that's not going to go over well with the crowd.

"*Hot Metal will be scratched from today's Travers . . .*"

The announcement goes floating over the stands to boos filling the air, while Hot Metal's jockey pulls the saddle off his gleaming back and the colt goes back to the stables with a hop in his step.

"Well, crap," Beck grumbles nearby.

"But isn't this a good thing?" Bri asks.

I nod. "It makes it easier," I admit. "But we wanted to beat Hot Metal. Looks like that will have to wait until later."

"Your bet is safer, though," Beck says. "Lucrative will have a hell of a better shot at hitting the board."

"Ah, but I didn't bet on Lucrative." Bri smiles while the horses reload, leaving it at that. When they break, she immediately yells for Quark Star, who muscles his way into fourth and sticks there in the middle of the pack as they race by the stands for the first time. A smile lights up on Beck, but then the rest is lost to the race. The group of colts does their best to make up for the loss of Hot Metal, as if everyone has renewed faith in their ability to win with the favorite out of the race.

The leader, a plucky bay colt with so-so breeding and a random race record, doesn't want to give in, even at the quarter mile pole with Star breathing down his neck. Everyone takes a stab at the front, and Jorge hesitates before pushing the button on Quark Star, the black colt almost getting swallowed by a tide of runners that are bound and determined to overtake the leader.

We're all shouting. I hear a nearby voice cussing up a storm at Jorge's lack of encouragement, but when it feels like we could all collectively wring the jockey's neck, Jorge twirls the whip in his fingers, brings it up and then flashes it down. Quark Star flies forward so fast there's a moment when I think he's bolting out of control. In three strides he's pulled out of the pack, and with a couple flicks of the crop, he's even with the bay. It's a matter of class that has Star rolling past and taking the Travers by two lengths.

Bri jumps up and down, holding her ticket and yelling, "What did I win? What did I win?"

Beck takes a look at it for her and then laughs. "Maybe a buck fifty?"

"Shut up, really?" Bri asks. The toteboard blinks the amounts as we walk down to the winner's circle, and Bri gets her pay out while we wait for our runner, who trots back fresh from his victory, covered in dirt but no worse for wear.

Chapter Fourteen

D elaney's post-Travers parties are not typically black-
tie affairs. Most of the time, you see Delaney himself sporting jeans, although his shoes are usually
leather and exceptionally shiny. For years the unspoken dress
code was the bare minimum that got you into a racetrack.
The results are always mixed. I was planning initially on
jeans, and maybe the nice shirt I've had hanging in my closest
the better part of the month. Bri takes one look at my plans
and shoots them all to hell.

"I don't think so," she says, making a sound of disapprov-
al and shoving the garment to the side. She immediately goes
for the dresses, rifling through them and pulling at the one I
haven't worn to the racetrack yet. I have it hidden in the back
of the closet, because it was a recent purchase that Bri encouraged. It's pretty, but it intimidates me, which seems silly
because it's only a stupid dress.

And yet it's not just a dress. It's a statement, which is
what Bri said when she pushed it in my hands and told me to
buy it. Statement dresses are short and sexy and strapless, not
to mention simple. I brought the red shoes to match the red
stripes that run around the bottom near the hem, and Bri
pulls them out of the closet triumphantly.

"Tonight is the night for that dress," she says, while I
look at it dubiously.

"I don't think you're hearing me when I say this is casual." I am pretty sure she is pretending I'm not talking.

"Who cares?" She puts the shoes on the bed, and I look at the heels with even more trepidation settling in my stomach. I've never worn those shoes in my life, just like the dress still has its tag and the receipt is still hidden in my room. It's something I haven't had the courage to wear, but haven't wanted to return. Bri rips the tag off the dress and fluffs out the skirt, grinning like a maniac.

"Come on, July."

"I don't know, Bri."

"Oh, for Christ's sake," Martina huffs from the doorway, one of her shoulders resting against the wood and her arms crossed over her chest with the air of an impatient governess. "Stop stalling. We'll be way past fashionably late if you keep this up."

"I'm not really concerned about punctuality, Martina," I snip at her, and she cocks her head to the side.

"Maybe not," she concedes, "but the last I checked, Beck likes blonds. And you weren't the one that was getting all the attention today."

"Oh my god," I say, ignoring the dress for a minute to focus on my sister's attitude. "Who do you think I am? Martina, if you hadn't noticed I am light years away from taking any sort of dating advice from you."

"Because you've never had the need," Martina says pointedly, her shoulders pushing back and settling against the door.

"No," I snap, "because I never had the inclination to throw myself at whoever happened across my path."

I know the instant I say it that I've made a huge mistake. Martina's whole face clouds over and she doesn't bother with a retort. She twirls around and is gone, leaving me with a hollow feeling. Bri shifts nervously.

"She was out of line," Bri says to me, and I shake my head.

"I think I kind of trumped that when I basically called her a whore."

Bri makes a face. "Yeah, maybe."

We don't say anything else, because the words may not be polite, but they're true. The first thing Martina did when we officially learned that Mom wasn't coming home was throw herself at Matthew Delaney. When whatever it was with Matthew fell to pieces, she picked herself up and trucked on to the next boy. It's been a pattern going on four years. Martina bounces from boy to boy, and I avoid them at all costs.

I look down at the dress and decide that I've done too much avoiding. After all, what do I have to show for eighteen years full of careful plans? Maybe Bri is right about a few things, and one of them is I should stop willingly sitting on the sidelines and pretending like I don't notice everything that goes on around me. Obviously, I notice. I think I notice too much.

Bri smiles when I pick up the dress and head for the bathroom. Before I can get there, Martina storms back up to my room and thrusts a scrap of material in my face. It's a strapless bra.

"You aren't flat-chested enough to pull that dress off without this," Martina says, like I shouldn't be trusted with my own wardrobe. "I don't need it tonight, so you can have it."

Weirdly enough, I am genuinely touched. Not because she's giving me a bra, but because she lost a war of words and didn't default to her standard reaction of storming off to her room and staying there until we're all gone. I am ridiculously proud of my big sister right now. I reach for her shoulder and pull myself up to her rigid body for a hug.

"Yeah, okay," she sighs. "Go put this stuff on so we can get your hair done and get over there already."

I think that's as close to apologies as we get in this family, so I follow orders and go.

At the party, the house is finally alive like it used to be, but it has a funny air to it, like people are here to gawk because they may not get another chance again. I should find something about this offensive, but I can't throw stones because I'm doing the same thing.

It's funny. I've spent several weeks wanting to know a sliver of what the future is going to hold, and here I am with dozens of other people wanting to know the same thing. It feels cheap, like we're all clambering to get a bit more before it's all gone.

I walk into the house with Bri on my heels, but she slips off almost immediately. I'm fine with that, really. It's a stretch to convince myself that Bri doesn't need someone to hold her hand with a group of people she doesn't know. She's Bri, and she'll be right as rain in any party.

I keep walking, snagging a drink and weaving in and out of crowds. Everyone is talking about the Travers, and Quark Star, and I find Jorge giving a group of women around him a lively rendition of racing the colt down the homestretch. I pause to listen to it, because Jorge isn't much for truthful re-tellings. Mostly everything is a drawn out exaggeration.

"What he isn't telling you," Beck says behind me, stealing all the attention, "is how often and loudly everyone in the stands was cursing him out for not firing sooner."

Of course, this only serves to puff up Jorge's extravagant retelling of the whole race. He smiles, and winks at the nearest girl. I roll my eyes and turn toward Beck.

"You're only encouraging him."

Beck only gives me a quiet, sure smile. "He doesn't need any help."

"And yet here you are."

"It's a guy thing."

"Sure it is," I say. "Where's your group of people?"

He shrugs. "I kind of didn't tell them about this."

"Why not?" I know the answer. It's hard enough having the whole community hovering around, waiting for Delaney to put a rest to their speculation. If rumor is anything to go by, tonight is the night for grand announcements, the ultimate speech for the ending of things. It's probably why the head count is higher than normal, even if you didn't count the fact that the first Blackbridge party is coming so late in the month. Usually we would've been through at least three by now.

Beck shifts his weight from foot to foot, like he's hopping on coals. "Want to go outside?"

"Are you planning on answering that question outside, or are you going to avoid it out there too?"

"You're being pretty direct today," he says, surprised. I shrug.

"I think we're at the point where someone should be."

I was hoping for a bit of a slip up on his part. Something that would make it easier for me to take the ball he's handed me and throw it forcefully back into his side of the court. It occurs to me that I hate sports analogies, especially now, because Beck's expression is blank. He's focusing on something else.

"Let's take a walk," he says, nodding to the doors to the back patio, which are open despite the running air conditioning. Humidity slides over me in a thick rush as soon as I set foot out of the house.

When we hit the plush carpet of grass, I wish I'd worn sensible shoes. I could curse Bri for this, and probably will later after I've inevitably fallen and sprained my abused ankle.

"You okay over there?" Beck asks me, watching me pick my way along in the dark.

"Fine," I say quickly. "Why do you ask?"

"No reason." I can hear the laughter in his voice, and I decide it's time to give up the charade, slipping off the shoes and sending him a look he can probably barely see from the light of the house. Of course, he sees enough.

"Comfortable?"

"Yes," I tell him, holding the heels in one hand and digging my toes into the grass. He's not moving anywhere, our walk seeming to end on the lawn between the main barn and the house. The training oval stretches in a giant yawn in front of us.

"So what are we doing out here?"

"Admittedly," he says through a sigh, "I didn't want to listen to Dad's routine in there."

"His routine," I echo. "Like what? Is his wandering around and sweet-talking innocent industry friends bothersome? I thought that was par for the course."

"No, actually," he says, shoving his hands in the pockets of his jeans. Jeans, I notice, while I stand next to him in this dress. The only effort he's taken to dress up his appearance is a white dress shirt he has loosely rolled up to the elbows, exposing the tanned skin of his forearms. I think about being self-conscious about this, but I really don't have it in me. "He's going to tell everyone his plans for the farm."

I go rigid, but Beck stops me before I can rush back to the house. "Juls, he's giving the bare minimum information. Like, it's been great to belong to this community, blah blah blah, we've got such phenomenal memories, blah blah, regretfully this is our last year, blah."

I'm quiet for a minute, because I'm trying to decide whether or not I should leave Beck in the grass and run back to the house in time to hear this admittedly less than inspirational speech. "Well, that's more than what most people have been willing to say so far, including you."

A shadow passes over his face, but it disappears as quick as it came.

"I told you about the failed investments," Beck says defensively.

"No, I mean what your parents are planning to do about it," I say. "The ramifications and what they mean."

"July," he says, looking me straight in the eye. It's dark, and I can barely make him out to know where he's looking, but I know. He's too still. "I think we all knew it was over in June."

"I didn't know."

"Well, you're not on the inside track."

"So tell me what being on the inside track is like," I challenge him, moving forward so I can see his face. It occurs to

180

me that I don't need to go back to the house. I have all the information I need in Beck, if only I can somehow pry it out of him.

"You don't want to know that," he says after a second of silence. "You want to know what's happening."

I stop myself from immediately commenting, because guilt floods through me and shuts me down faster than I can speak. It's not only my life that's radically going to change if everything I think might happen actually does. Beck is more affected than I am. Dad will have clients beating down his door in a matter of days, but Beck's family will have to rebuild.

"I want to know both," I amend, stumbling on my words. "Tell me both."

He's still silent. Fine. New tactic.

"Okay," I let out a breath. "I'm sorry. It's been on my mind for a while."

"We're selling," he blurts out, like he hasn't even heard me all this time. I imagine that's probably the case.

"What do you mean?"

"I mean we're selling," he says simply. "The farm, the horses, even the Fifth Avenue apartment, because my parents can't figure out how to justify keeping it. Anything that isn't necessary is going, July. For a while, we're going to be a one-home family. Can you imagine?"

"That isn't funny, Beck," I say, not quite sure if I'm referencing his quip or the whole thing.

He gives me a pained grimace, and then stares blankly out at the training oval. "I'm not saying it is."

I stand and look at him for a moment, processing. So it's as bad as I had thought after all, although I can't help the questions that keep cropping up, like persistent weeds I can't cut back.

"All the horses?" I ask quietly, keeping my gaze on his profile as he stands with his hands in his pockets, pretending to be relaxed. "Galaxy and Star and . . ."

"Diver and even that Kali horse you like so much, yes."

I swallow down a hard lump in my throat, thinking how ironic it is that I never wanted to give up the horses. I hated the very idea of sending Kali into a claimer, as if we don't do those sorts of things every month, and here the truth is staring me in the face. All the horses are going. None of them will be saved, and this ending is absolute. Blackbridge is finished.

My mind veers off in a new direction and settles on the last thing I would have expected.

"What about Lighter?"

He's quiet for a minute, transferring his gaze from the track down to his shoes. "I own Lighter."

I want to reach out and squeeze his wrist, just to get more of a response out of him. I stay where I am, wallowing in my questions and my insecurities. Then another particularly painful wave of guilt crashes over my head, battering it home that this is more than the horses. This is Beck's life that is slipping down the drain. I let out a breath I wasn't aware of holding.

"What about you?"

He laughs, but it's not reassuring. If anything he sounds upset, like he's spent a lot of time thinking about this and come to conclusions he doesn't much like. He lifts his gaze from his shoes and looks right at me. "That's the glory of trust funds. I'll be fine."

He hasn't convinced me, so he adds. "Not great, but fine. And if I need to, I've got a future Hopeful Stakes winner. What do you think a potential Breeders' Cup Juvy starter will bring?"

"That's really not funny," I say, not laughing. "He's not a Hopeful winner, Beck."

At that, he really does laugh. Loud and lively, like there's real humor in it. "Leave it to you to be that practical."

"He isn't," I say insistently. "Not yet. So don't sell him yet. Wait until he wins."

His laughter dies out. I hear things quieting down in the house, which seems like a long way from us right now. The music has been shut off, and there are less people milling around the porch. Beck considers me thoughtfully, as if I've said the last thing he expected.

"You think he can win the Hopeful?"

I'm an honest person. Sometimes I let my deluded thought process get in the way, but I know what that colt is capable of. "Yes."

He nods. "Well, that's something."

The house is quiet. It's nagging at me, making me uncomfortable. I finally reach out for Beck's hand and pull him closer to the solitude of the barns. He lets me tug him along, his hand moving to grasp mine as my heart beats out a quick rhythm and I force myself to take steady steps. I see Maggie grazing near the fence closest to the gravel lot, the white splotches of her coat standing out in the dark.

"What about school?" I ask, walking next to him, the grass whispering and crunching under my bare feet. There will be grass stains on my skin later.

"I don't think it's that bad," he says. "I'm not going to become a homeless, uneducated jackass who happens to own a racehorse."

"What *about* your racehorse?" I ask. "Where will Lighter go?"

"If I don't sell him, he'll stay with your dad," Beck says with a shrug. "Why make your life any easier?"

I pause, because hearing some life rush back into Beck is a relief. "You're not being as cute as you think you are."

"Sure I am," he responds. "I'm adorable."

"Uh-huh."

"I am pretty sure I'm not the only one here who thinks so."

Have you ever tried to stop blushing? It's uncommonly hard. Actually, it's more like impossible. I give up and do the verbal equivalent of running for cover.

"That's because you think too highly of yourself."

"July," he says, "I can't help but base my own self-image on the information others have given me."

"Then you're surrounded by sycophants," I say easily.

He grins. "I'm really not."

"It's too bad your friends didn't stick around," I say, thinking of the skinny blond with her huge sunglasses and her smile meant only for Beck. "Then I'd probably find out more to prove you wrong. In fact, I bet Ms. Sunglasses would have an interesting opinion I would absolutely love to hear."

Beck opens his mouth to say something and seems to think better of it. Instead he says, "Jealous?"

I would love to know what he was going to say, because I'm pretty sure if I could see his eyes they'd be glittering in amusement. "I'm right, aren't I?" I ask, neatly avoiding his succinct question and trying to ignore the fact that he's still holding onto my hand.

"You know," he says, ignoring me. "If you are jealous, that's totally okay. I've got some experience in this area, and I think I can successfully talk you out of doing something hasty."

"You are such an asshole," I say, smacking him in the chest. He's too busy laughing to care. "And I am absolutely right."

"If you're right and I include you in with them, doesn't that cast a bad light on you?"

"Not if I don't qualify myself as your friend," I say, eyeing him and wondering what I'm saying. Sometimes I don't know why I say the things I do. It's got something with talking before I think, and I do it too much around Beck. It's like I fall into a wordy maelstrom around him, and it must be stopped at all costs.

"So what do you qualify yourself as?" he asks, watching me intensely. I tell myself to think before I answer, but the first thing that pops into my head is what slips through my mouth.

"The girl you kiss in order to get back at her." Damn it. He's entirely too pleased.

I have to do something, and I have to do it quickly. If I don't he'll say something I don't want to hear, like how sweet it is that I'm hung up on him. Him, of all people. And then I'll do something stupid in response, like punch him in the arm and take off for the house, Delaney speech or no, like we're twelve all over again.

So in a split second, right when I see the bright glint in his eye transform into a thought that is about to make its way out into the open air, I pull myself haphazardly forward, sink my fingers into his shirt, and yank him the rest of the way toward me.

Not knowing what I'm doing isn't really a critical factor. I don't know what I'm doing, because I've never done this. I don't want to get preoccupied with whether or not I'm doing it right, because I don't want to think that much right now.

Beck drags his feet through the grass, complete shock falling over him to my total delight, right before we come at each other awkwardly. My mouth meets his, and I have to rise up on my toes to get there when he doesn't have the forethought to bring himself down to my level. It doesn't take him long, and my heels find their way back to the grass when he leans down and pulls me closer, breaking off the kiss for a second so we can stare at each other while I breathe too rapidly underneath his chin.

"That was well played," he admits, and I would thump him on the chest, but he still has me pressed there.

"Please no more sports metaphors," I say. "I really don't think this is the time or the place."

"I can do that." He lifts one hand from my hip and settles it on the back of my neck, tipping me into him. I press myself into him willingly, lift an arm around his neck to get closer, so we can do this frenzied, warm thing I've wanted, but never done.

"I'm sorry," I find myself saying against his lips, and he gives me a quizzical look.

He kisses me and says, "Why?"

"For Blackbridge."

"It's not the end of the world," he says. "Besides, we've got Lighter."

I laugh, feeling this thing in my stomach that's making me giddy. He kisses me again, and I lean back, letting the arm he has wrapped around my back serve as support. I pull back and say, "Because Lighter is going to win the Hopeful."

"Damn straight Lighter is going to win the Hopeful," he says, and we're both grinning like idiots, watching each other from only inches away. "By the way," he continues, moving his thumb in these maddening circles against the material of my dress. "Nothing is going on with Ms. Sunglasses. I thought I'd tell you so you aren't feeling some moral quandary over making out with someone who's taken."

"Thanks," I say, rolling my eyes. "That really clears my conscience."

"Thought so." He kisses me, and everything is warm, verging on hot. It's long and sweet, deepening until little tingles drip along every nerve right down to my fingertips. I don't know how I can hear with all the blood rushing in my ears. Nevertheless, I do, and it resembles a hard, muted thud. I pull back, my lips hot and deliciously damp.

"Did you . . ." I start, stopping when I hear it again. It sounds like flesh hitting wood, and then a scrape of metal. Beck lets me go.

"Is anyone with the horses?" he asks, and I drop the shoes on the grass, toeing into them and rising an unsteady three inches.

"I don't know," I say, heading toward the barn. "Come on."

The doors to the barn are open, because it's summer and the horses appreciate the occasional breeze if they're not out in the paddocks. I turn on all the overhead lights, which blink to life and flood the whole barn. A few curious horses stick their heads over their stall doors, pricking their ears at us as we make our way down the aisle.

Beck starts checking each stall. I take the opposite side of the barn, casting a glance at each dozing horse. When I get to Lighter, he lays his ears back at me and shifts his weight, but that's nothing new. More than likely he's just upset that his beauty rest has been disturbed.

"How's your side?" I ask, moving past Lighter's stall.

"Fine," Beck says. "So far."

I hear another bump and then a riot of thrashing, the sound of hooves scraping down wood sending me scrambling up the aisle. Before, I would have said I couldn't run in three-inch heels. I know I can now, because I sprint down the concrete and come to an abrupt halt outside Diver's stall.

Beck comes to a skidding halt next to me, taking one look over my shoulder and saying, "Shit."

Diver is twisted over on the ground, his hooves a chaotic tangle against the wall of his stall. His sides are heaving, and he has his neck and head stretched out as far as it can go. He's resting on the shavings, but his eyes are wild and his normally light gray coat is dark all over with sweat. I have no idea how long he's been like this, but there's no way we can let him go a second longer when he's almost sprawled on his back.

"We need to get my dad," I say quickly, letting myself into the stall. I take a look down at my shoes and wish I had time to change, but this is Diver. There's no time for appropriate footwear. "We need to get him on his feet."

"Rope?" Beck asks, beginning to edge for the tack room, but I shake my head.

"No," I say. The gelding is staring at us, beginning to twist some more against the wall. "At least, not yet. He's calm right now. We can grab his legs and tip him over."

"Okay," Beck says, walking up behind me and moving over to Diver's hind legs. "Just don't get kicked in the head, all right?"

"You too," I manage to say, leaning down and putting one hand on Diver's neck, mumbling wordless noises to him as I press my hand down his shoulder and up his nearest front leg. I grasp his fetlock, and glance over at Beck, who has a firm hold on Diver's left hind.

"We don't need to do much," I say. "Just pull and let gravity take him the rest of the way."

Beck nods. "On three?"

"Sure."

I tighten my hold on Diver's leg and pull. The gelding makes a surprised grunt, but doesn't start thrashing. Beck makes a noise similar to the gelding, and before I know it I'm tugged back while Diver's legs go falling in front of my face.

"Thanks," I say, breathless as I look down at Beck's hands wrapped around my waist, and then at Diver, who is starting to get himself sorted out.

"Yeah," he says right back. "Next time, do what you say you're going to do. For a second, I thought you were going to let him roll right over you."

"Wow, big hero you are."

He smiles, and I slip out of his grasp, kneeling down by Diver's head. "We've got to get him up."

"He won't do it himself?"

I take a second, and then finally say it. "Not if he's colicking."

Beck pauses for a beat. "Fantastic. You push, I'll pull."

Beck grabs the halter's cheekpiece and pulls, lifting the gelding's head while I push from behind, shoving Diver's neck and shoulder until he gets his legs stretched in front of him and he hauls himself up. We finally have him standing between us, and I let out a breath in sheer relief. Shavings are sticking to my sweaty skin, and I think more than a few have gotten into my shoes. I repress the urge to kick them off, because there's more work to do.

"Okay, now we need his lead."

Beck goes to get it, while I lead Diver to the aisle by his halter. It's slow going, and I wonder if he's thinking about dropping to the concrete to roll. Diver turns in on himself, focusing on something internal and too perplexing for his poor brain to compute. It has to be colic. I can see nothing else wrong with him besides his scrapped up legs.

I run my hand over Diver's side, try to listen and feel for anything that would prove me wrong. His belly is firm and quiet.

Beck comes back with the lead rope and hands it over.

"I'm going to try to take him for a walk in the parking lot," I tell him. "I've got to keep him on his feet, Beck . . ."

"Hey," he says, nodding as he grabs my wrist, squeezing lightly. "I'll get your dad."

Diver drops his nose almost to the ground, preferring to plant his face in the concrete than take a step. I see his knees begin to buckle and jump to drag him forward. He stumbles, steadies, and lurches after me.

I want to be relieved, but I'm shivering and nervous. Diver falters again, and I pull him forward, breaking Beck's hold.

"Go," I tell him, and watch as he runs off into the night.

Chapter Fifteen

"**O**kay, friend, here's the deal."

Diver walks next to me as I finish up the third circuit around the parking lot. The gravel is loose under my shoes and making me wobble as I walk. Diver won't lift his head up past my elbow, and he takes periodic breaks to attempt sinking to his knees. He's trying to get down on the ground and roll, one of the few ways horses have of relieving the pain caused by blockage in their guts. It's a misplaced effort, usually ending in twisted and ruptured intestines. It's a slow, awful death.

I tug on the lead rope and teeter on a loose stone, catching myself and pulling us both forward.

"You're going to walk around with me just a little longer," I say to Diver, "and before you know it all of this is going to be over. Then I'll take you to Woodfield, where you'll live the high life."

I pause, trying to pick a persistent piece of Diver's bedding out of my shoe. The gelding stalls next to me, standing on braced legs while I dig out the shaving from under my heel and start walking again. He follows without any of his usual determination.

"I know you're thinking there have to be better places than an acre paddock and an old barn," I say, filling the quiet air. "But you've never been there before so I don't think you should judge until you see it."

I'm babbling, but I can't make myself shut up. If I've learned anything over the years, it's that horses do listen to you. They may not have a clue what you're saying, but they know the tone in which you say it. I'll sing to horses so hooked on their own nerves they're ready to climb into the sky, and sometimes it's one of the only things that keep them on the ground. With Diver, I want to keep him distracted, soothed, but following an order. And the order is move, whether he likes it or not.

I look over my shoulder as we pass by the track, and see a small contingent of people hurrying over the lawn. Dad's lanky form leads the group, which I notice includes Bri and Martina. Gus and Izzie are in tow, sporting mirroring worried expressions. Then there's Beck and Delaney himself, which puts my heart in my throat.

We're going to face a big decision with Diver tonight. Delaney's presence guarantees it.

Dad reaches me first.

"Hold up, July."

I stop walking, and Diver turns his head into my knee. His muzzle presses there, warm against my skin, and I reach down to comb my fingers through his forelock. If I could will this horse to get better, I would. We have plans, he and I.

Dad asks routine questions that I answer, watching him lift up Diver's lips to get a look at the gelding's gums. His fingers aren't in Diver's mouth more than a second before the gelding literally falls to the ground.

I jump, and a strangled yelp claws its way up my throat. The sound of a horse falling onto gravel is sickening, but seeing it happen right in front of you is something else altogether. I move to Diver's head, but Dad cuts me off at the pass, taking the lead rope out of my hands while Diver paws ineptly at the jagged rocks, trying to roll or escape or both.

I see Bri with her hands pressed to her mouth. Martina hovers behind her, gaping at the scene unfolding at her feet. Beck lifts his eyes from the gelding to me, and I can tell exactly what he's thinking the second I catch his gaze.

I'm not prepared to agree with him.

"Where's the vet, Dad?" I ask, irritated at Delaney for shaking his head silently at the horse, like he's made up his mind already.

"We called from the house," he says, but he's not looking at me. Instead he looks up at Delaney and says, "This might be a surgical case. We'll leave him on the ground until the vet gets here. July," he redirects to me, "get him up if he starts to roll. I don't want this to be totally catastrophic if we can help it. This is already screwed beyond belief."

Diver halfheartedly digs at the gravel, lifting his head and thunking it on the ground. I sink down to my knees beside him and arrange his head in my lap, firmly putting my hands on his neck to still him. Diver allows this, letting out a shuddering breath against my dress. I stroke my hands over his neck, trace down his face, rub them over his ears. He calms, one big brown eye gazing up at the night sky.

For a second, I think about Mom and about the way she used to ride this horse. I think about her bending over his neck in the saddling paddock and whispering into his flying mane.

I swallow with difficulty, tears beginning to swim in my eyes and stuffing up my throat. Mom always had a blind sort of faith about Diver. He ran for himself as much as he did it for her.

He takes care of me out there, she'd said, and I had always believed her.

I card my fingers through Diver's forelock and lean over him, murmuring soft words.

Dios te salve, Maria. Llena eres de gracia: El Señor es contigo.

He pricks his ears, like he must remember. So I say the rest.

Bendita tú ere entre todas las mujeres. Y bendito es el fruto de tu vientre: Jesús. Santa María, Madre de Dios, ruega por nosotros pecadores, ahora y en la hora de nuestra muerte.

Amén.

When I finish, the vet is rolling up in a sparkling rig. I wipe at my eyes, and watch as Diver is pumped full of painkillers. His eyes become glassy and his head becomes heavier in my lap.

"He's going to the clinic," Beck says, walking up to me while my father and Delaney confer with the vet. Izzie and Gus stand nearby, waiting to be of use in getting Diver to his feet. Martina and Bri still huddle together a few yards away, done with the party. I don't blame them. It would be hard to go back to having fun after watching a horse dying in a gravel lot.

"What else?"

"Nothing else." Beck shrugs. "We're going to try to save him."

I don't say anything. I'm thankful, really. As a gelding, Diver isn't the best investment. If he survives, he's unlikely to come back to the racetrack, although I've heard weirder stories. It's just that every time I feel Diver breathe a cold reality settles into my stomach.

"Beck," Delaney says, breaking off from the group. "We'll need your help here."

"Same for you, July," Dad says, putting a hand on my shoulder. "I need to you guide him."

He helps me climb out from under Diver, and hands me the gelding's lead. Beck and Dad rouse Diver to his feet, pushing on his shoulder and hindquarters, but he wants nothing to do with standing. Gus and Delaney join in, applying needed pressure. There's a steady string of curses from the men, and I brace myself to pull as Diver swings his head up, eyes finally gone crazy, and twists to get his feet under him.

"Come on," I call to him. "Up, up!"

Diver launches himself to his feet so forcefully he almost falls back down. Beck jumps out of the way, but comes back to lean support into the gelding's hindquarters. The gelding wavers amongst all of our hands. Dad and Gus link arms under his tail, keeping him from backing away from the rig that I direct him toward.

I keep up my cheery encouragement as I back toward the rig. Diver watches me intently, so focused on me that I have to swallow a lump in my throat. When one of my ruined heels touches the ramp, I turn and I trot into the trailer next to his unsteady walk.

It's there that I take a moment to breathe, touching my forehead to his neck.

Izzie squeezes in next to me, taking the lead rope. "I'm going to escort this guy to the clinic," she says, beginning to tie the gelding up. "You need to go home. Rest."

I nod slowly, forehead still pressed against Diver's coat.

Izzie tugs me back down the ramp, and I fall into Bri, who grabs onto me in a bear hug.

"He'll be okay," Bri says when the gelding is secure in the trailer and the big metal doors clang shut behind him.

I don't let go.

~~

In the morning, I muck out Diver's stall. The gelding isn't coming back to it, so I get rid of everything. Once I have the bedding and the feed tubs out of this space, I figure it will really hit home.

Bri stands outside the stall. Her tote bag is nearly falling off her shoulder and her keys are in her hand, her face screwed up in a contortion of disbelief and pity. I keep shoveling bedding until the metal spade hits the floor, and I scrape at it, getting everything up and into the wheelbarrow waiting outside. My hands hurt through the gloves from gripping the wooden handle too hard, but I don't really mind it. It's a bit of a reminder; yes, I'm alive. No, Diver isn't.

"I'm sorry," Bri says again, but I shake my head.

"It's not your fault. These things," I say, feeling the empty stall behind me more than I'd like, to the point that I fall silent. I cough into my gloves and force a smile. "They happen."

Bri frowns, crossing her arms over her chest. "Come on," she says, "I know he was going to be yours."

"Maybe he would have been mine," I say, catching a sniffle. I wipe at my eyes. Bri pulls me into a hug without thought, resting her head against mine. We stand there in the aisle while I pull myself together.

I've never been too good at this. We lose horses. They're sold, they're transferred, they're retired, and they die. Not one of them is ever a permanent fixture, but I'm well aware that nothing in this life is ever a sure thing. Sometimes I want something stable, and I wonder why it is that I've been building up so much on a rickety foundation.

I pull away from Bri. "You're going to be late getting back."

She shrugs. "No big. I'm leaving for the beach this week, and what do I have to do other than a ton of laundry and packing and errands?"

"Right," I say, breaking into a real smile for her. "Because you can do all of that in your sleep."

"I'm very efficient," Bri says, shrugging like this is a simple fact of her life. "You should really consider my offer, by the way."

"Offer?"

Bri rolls her eyes. "Has it been that long since you've had a vacation?"

Ah. I cock my head to the side and ask, "Vacation?"

"Okay," Bri says, "I distinctly remember wanting you to come to the Outer Banks with me. You know, it's a beach. There's lots of sand there, and an ocean. It's perfect for things like doing nothing and catching up on trashy novels."

"Well, when you say it like that," I say, resting the shovel on the wheelbarrow and tugging at my gloves so they fit better over my fingers. Bri raises an eyebrow, like she's waiting for me to agree with her and run up to the loft to get my things. Right about now, I would like to do just that, but Diver's empty stall is still a nagging void behind me and I can't. Not right now, if ever.

"It sounds great, Bri," I say.

She sighs. "But?"

"But," I begin, "this is my last year here with Blackbridge. It's something I have to do."

Bri nods. "Then I guess I accept defeat. This means you're obligated to come with me on any spring break trip of my choosing, which we are definitely doing, because there is no way you can juggle NYU and Belmont Park at the same time, right?"

"If I'm enrolled by then," I say. "And technically, it would be Aqueduct at that point."

"Okay, shut up," Bri laughs. "You're going."

"Understood," I say. "Spring break is on."

"Good," Bri says, giving me another hug again. "And if you change your mind about the Outer Banks, say so. You're welcome to show up whenever."

"Thanks," I say, although it's muffled by her shoulder and the blouse she's wearing. Bri pulls back and I walk her out to the car, Bri hauling her last huge suitcase and me pushing the wheelbarrow full of Diver's soiled bedding. We look odd together, but that's nothing new. Bri wrestles the suitcase into the trunk of her car and makes a face. "Okay," she says, "maybe I did pack too much."

"I'd like to see what you bring to North Carolina," I say, laughing when she sends a glare in my direction.

"Some of us aren't as decisive as you," Bri says, which is such a lie.

"Right," I say. "Get on the road now, before I find something for you to do in the barn."

"I'm going," Bri says, wrinkling her nose in distaste at the idea of mucking out stalls. I don't blame her a bit. She hops into her car and the engine roars to life. Seconds later, she rolls down her window and yells, "Call me!"

"Will do," I say, waving her off. I watch her car crawl carefully across the gravel drive to the main road, and finally disappear altogether. That's that, I think, and push the wheelbarrow down to the manure heap, dumping the last of it.

～

People have a way of thinking that tomorrow will be better. I think that the people who say this have no idea what they're talking about. The day after Diver dies, Kali is in a claimer. Twenty thousand dollars could buy her as soon as she's out of the gate. Right now, I could say something about how experience has taught me not to take this too personally. That's too bad, because currently my heart is in my throat and there's no hope of dislodging it any time soon.

"You look like you're about to vomit," Martina informs me while we stand in the saddling paddock. Kali dances around by Izzie's shoulder, her pretty bronze head bobbing and her white feet stamping out an excited storm. She looks like she wants to run, and run well. If I were someone with cash to burn and no knowledge of racing, I'd want to buy her, and this thought makes me nervous.

"I've put some work into her this summer," I say tonelessly to Martina. "I guess it's gotten emotional for me."

"Which is why you shouldn't have been spending so much time riding her," Martina shrugs. "You knew she'd be back in a claimer by the end of the summer."

Easy for her to say, I guess. It's also true; I did know Kali would be in a claimer before we left Saratoga. I started riding her anyway. Nevertheless, I don't want to dignify that with a response, so I walk over to Beck, who has his hands in his pockets and his eyes trained on his feet. He looks about as happy as I feel.

"Today sucks," I inform him.

His mouth quirks in an attempt at a smile before he seems to abandon the effort. "Yeah, it really does. Hopefully your pony over there will stick out the rest of the meet with us."

I let out a breath. "She's not my pony."

"Well, no," Beck says, "but maybe I just don't want to lose another horse so soon."

Maybe once, a short while ago, I would have called him out on his caring about a filly like Kali considering he couldn't remember her name at the start of the summer. Instead I think about Diver, about the lack of Diver, and don't say anything at all.

The race is a mile, once around the course. Kali rates in fourth the whole way around until the end, when the crowd of horses starts to move and leaves her behind. Pilar gets her moving at the quarter pole with twenty-some-odd seconds left in the race. Kali jumps like she's been bitten on the ass and swings wide from the group.

"Oh, hell," I say through a sigh, watching the filly while Pilar works to get her straight and running toward the finish line. Kali uncoils and finally goes at the one-eighth pole, in fifth and chasing a very determined set of horses.

Pilar gives her a few more pops with the whip, and Kali gives a true effort this time. I can see it, despite the fact that she's racing down the middle of the track with no hope of hitting the board. The filly's got her ears back, her stride is sure, she's doing what Pilar wants her to do for a change. The problem is she's just so terribly untalented.

Then the two horse stumbles, falling right onto her face and flipping her jockey clear over her shoulder as she somersaults into Kali's path. To the stunned gasps of onlookers, Kali dives to the outside and leaps into the air, putting Pilar up on her neck in efforts to get clear. She lands awkwardly, and that's it for Pilar, who rolls onto the dirt and lands like a flopping doll.

Kali gets all four feet underneath her and goes charging off after the rest of the horses, her reins flapping wildly around her neck. Her strides are even and sure, but the filly is panicked, running loose. If she gets one foot through the loop of her reins, she'll be done for.

I immediately move to push my way out of the box, but Beck and Martina grab at me.

"Stay," Martina orders, while my father and his entourage file out to deal with the situation.

"I don't think so," I argue, struggling out of their gasps and rushing down to the track, my heart high in my throat as I elbow my way through the crowd.

It seems to take forever to catch up with Dad, but once I do, I run past him.

"Juls," he starts, but I shake my head, not listening.

"It's Kali, Dad," I shout over my shoulder, catching his shifting expression. He nods once, and quickens his pace behind me. Kali may be our problem child, but she's still ours. And until she's anything different, I'm going to do my best to make sure she gets home safe.

Even if my best isn't much at all.

I plunge out onto the harrowed dirt, my heels sinking into the soft surface. An ambulance is sitting further up the track, its lights off. The two horse is up, all four hooves planted solidly on the ground as a vet looks over her legs. Pilar is sitting on the dirt, her arm cradled to her chest and wet lines streaking down her cheeks as she nods at a medic.

I can't hear anything, and it occurs to me that I don't know what I can hope to accomplish until I spot Kali, who dodges away from an outrider and bolts the wrong way down the outside rail, headed back for the grandstand.

"Juls!" Martina yells, pushing her way up to the rail with Beck close behind. I shake my head at them and turn toward Kali, who rushes toward me. I hold out my arms, lift them over my head, and reach out for her as she comes to a sweaty, exhausted halt.

"Good job, girl," I whisper to her, wrapping an arm around her damp neck as she lowers her head and presses against my dress.

Now the crowd cheers.

I look up, noticing Martina trooping toward me, her heels making pointy marks in the dirt. Beck comes up and undoes Pilar's saddle, hauling it off Kali's steaming back. She seems undamaged, which I think must be a miracle until the ambulance drives by and I remember that Pilar is hurt.

"What do we know about Pilar?" I ask, spinning around when Dad comes up to take the saddle, handing it off to his assistant so he can check Kali's legs.

"Broken arm," says Dad, lifting Kali's right fore to study a small scrape on her fetlock. Beck winces, and I know he's thinking about who will ride Lighter in the Hopeful. "But this girl," Dad pats Kali's shoulder, "is fine."

I breathe out a relieved sigh.

Izzie appears with a bucket of water, dousing Kali liberally over her back and chest while I hold her. More steam rises, and Kali shakes herself, dotting me with warm water droplets. That's when I see a woman holding a red tag in her hand at the rail, waiting on the horses to come back to the grandstand. The red tag means a horse was claimed, and when she finds the particular horse she'll attach the red square to the bridle.

"I want to be sick," I say, and am rewarded with a worried glance from Martina. Beck's hand on my back rubs a soft circle between my shoulder blades. I try to focus on the warmth he's generating, but it's no good.

"Hey," he says, as Izzie gently takes Kali's reins from my fingers and begins to walk the filly in cooling circles, "if something happens, we'll figure it out. She doesn't fall into some void afterward."

I smile, feeling a flash of hopeless relief. "Thanks," I say. "That means a lot."

It's also so freakishly unrealistic. We both know that. Beck shrugs, like this offhanded magnanimous offer is typical of him. I want to laugh, but my stomach is so tight I think I really will be sick.

"There," Martina says, pointing to the number four horse. "She's going after the gray."

I'm not satisfied until I see the tag on the gray's bridle and Kali is safe, for the moment. I can't get better confirmation than that.

"See?" Beck says, close to my ear. "Safe."

The thing is, while I watch Kali follow Izzie to the backside, all I can see is Diver. All I can feel is the regret of not asking Delaney more, pushing for more, attaining a result. Diver deserved that stall at Woodfield, just like Kali can be more than a Saratoga claimer.

Just like that, I'm done with it. The merry-go-round of claimers, the anxiety, and the ceaseless attempts to get Kali to be something she never wanted to be. Kali is not a racer.

She can be more. I know it, and I know I can get her there.

Chapter Sixteen

I realize that I never had a plan with Diver. It was more like a handful of halfhearted hopes, because somewhere down deep I was never too sure I was going to wedge him out from this life. It would have to be easier now, wouldn't it? Diver was a stakes winner, a horse with a following. What is Kali other than a collection of dismal efforts and a few pretty workout times? What does Delaney want with a pitiful morning glory?

He doesn't want her. This is why I've got this fluttering feeling in my chest, this optimism I can't shake. I really should kick it to the curb for the time being, because I'm riding Lighter and you'd think I'd learn by now that letting my mind wander with this colt is like willingly stepping in front of a firing squad.

We're standing in one of the stalls in the saddling paddock at Saratoga, getting Lighter accustomed to the sights and smells so there's less chance he'll have sensory overload on Hopeful day. Normally Pilar would be riding Lighter during his paddock training, but instead she's leaning against the rail with her arm in a bright white cast, yelling at me when I make a wrong move.

"Don't let him get away with that, Juls," she calls at me from her spot next to Dad, shaking her head as Lighter tries to rub me up against the sides of the stalls. I give him a nudge and he corrects, huffing excitedly.

Just to make things more realistic, Beck helpfully pierces the air with one of those ear-shattering whistles. Lighter hunches and leaps sideways underneath me, trying to turn and dart. When I bring him back to himself, he shivers and lowers his face into the bridle, hauling on my arms like the jerk he is.

"Thanks a lot," I yell over at Beck, who's sitting sprawled out on a bench near the paddock. He smiles and nods, giving me this lackadaisical two-finger salute before going back to stretching his arms over the back of the bench. If I fall off and onto one of the many hard objects in this paddock, I am definitely making him ride his idiot horse for the rest of the year.

That might be an empty threat. Whatever.

Martina glares at him from her spot on the bench and crosses her legs primly, turning back to the copy of the *Daily Racing Form* that's unfolded over her knees. I turn my attention back to Lighter, who is busy dancing around next to Gus as we take another cruise through the paddock. I'm hoping this is the last lap of the day, because things have worked out so far and I don't want to push our luck.

Except a chipmunk has to go ruin those plans. It darts out onto the walkway, pauses in terror at the behemoth prancing toward it, and does a hysterical circle before coming to a brief stop to squeak belligerently. That's a lot of gall for a chipmunk. Lighter, of course, completely flips out. With a squeal of indignant outrage, he lunges at it. The chipmunk darts out of sight, back to the bushes, but Lighter's on a roll. He rears and comes down, rears higher and comes down. I grip onto his mane, feeling the cracking thunk of his front hooves meeting the walkway every time we connect with the earth again.

Gus gets him moving, saying something very firm in Spanish that goes right over my head. Lighter does an excited plunging maneuver around him until he comes to a quivering halt in the grass somewhere in the vicinity of the pathway. Now I'm the one shivering, and a hunk of Lighter's blond mane is twisted in my fingers, ripped way from his neck in my efforts to hold on.

"Nice bit of riding," Gus says to me through his Spanish discussion with Lighter, who is listening intently, but probably still on the lookout for the chipmunk.

"Nice bit of hanging on for dear life, you mean," I correct him, wincing as I shake Lighter's mane from my fingers and watch it drift to the ground. "Thanks for holding on."

Gus snorts at that and lifts his hand to Lighter's face, stroking down the colt's forehead while Lighter looks intently at the bushes. With a few short words in Spanish from Gus, reprimands most likely, and a few definite curses, we're off again.

"Hey, July? Is this a moment when I should apologize for my horse?"

I wish I were close enough so I could at least hit him on the shoulder. "Shut up, Beck," I say, making the turn toward the saddling stalls so I can see him and Martina sitting there on their bench. Beck is grinning, because I guess me being manhandled by his horse is funny for him, and Martina is giving him the most disgusted glare she can come up with. Eventually she reaches over and smacks his knee with the back of her hand. He jumps and says something I can't hear to Martina, who rolls her shoulders and goes back to her paper.

I smile to myself, happy to see my sister right on the same page with me.

Lighter floats back into his stall, his nearly white tail swishing and his whole body screaming sassiness. I guess physically threatening a rodent is high on his list of achievements. I jump off of him before he can add throwing me over his shoulder for the umpteenth time onto that list.

Gus doesn't give Lighter a second to think about anything once I'm successfully on the ground, and leads the colt back around the stalls and toward the backside, where our trailer is ready to take us all back to Blackbridge. Dad gives us a casual nod of acknowledgement from the rail, and I don't know exactly what that means because he's glued to his cell phone.

I plop down on the bench by Martina, who is glaring at the paper. Beck is reading something over her shoulder, his eyebrows furrowed in concentration. Finally, Martina shoves the pages together in a flurry of crinkled noise and shoves them all at me. I look down at the rumpled newsprint in my lap and don't have a chance to even sort it out before Beck is grabbing it from me, smoothing out the wrinkles and going back to the page Martina was reading with all the fury of a person with a cause.

"What's going on?" I ask. Martina jumps up and whirls to face me.

"You didn't read that?"

Oh, for the love of Christ. "Of course I haven't read it," I say. "I've been riding horses all morning. What is your problem?"

Martina stews in front of me, crossing her arms and glaring because she doesn't believe me.

"Don't give me that crap, July. You can't be trusted to know normal news, but you'll absorb everything from the printed word to gossip if it involves racing."

"Okay," I say slowly, shrugging because this is the last outburst I expected. "I haven't gotten to it yet. You'll have to be satisfied with that answer, because I don't know what else to tell you."

I hear crumpling paper to my left, where Beck is folding the *Form* and handing it over to me. "First article on the page, three paragraphs down," is all he says to me when I take it.

I begin to scan over the words, slipping into routine. I rove over the lines and letters, coming to a dead halt when I hit *Celia Carter*. My fingertips go cold, but I force myself on. *Celia Carter*, the paper tells me.

Celia Carter and *Saratoga* and *Hopeful*.

∿

When I started to obsessively read all those papers and programs, I never really knew what I'd do when I found her name. Oh, sure, freaking out is a completely valid response, but it's just a reaction. I never knew what I would *do*, after I'd gotten over the knowledge that this would happen and there was nothing I could do to stop it. Would I want to stop it? Would I want to hunt her down? Would I petulantly lurk in the shadows, torturing myself with glimpses? What would I do?

My mother sure as hell is not coming to me. I realized that this spring, when she appeared and disappeared at Aqueduct without so much as saying a word.

This news makes an uncomfortable ride back to Black-bridge. Lighter knocks his hoof repetitively against the side of the rig, while Martina grills Dad in a method that is impressive, bordering on obsessive. Beck has his head tipped toward the ceiling, adam's apple bobbing each time he swallows, eyes closed like he's in some other world. I keep reading the article, over and over and over. My eyes stick on the words every time.

Celia Carter and Saratoga and Hopeful.

"This doesn't mean she'll be here," I say, my voice shrill to be heard over Martina's incessant arguing and Dad's rapidly disintegrating patience. Martina swings around to pin her eyes on me, like she'd rather snap my fledgling hopes in half than waste her time telling me they have no chance of making it into the world.

"Tell me what that article says," she demands, and my slight pause makes her reach into the backseat to rip the paper out of my hands so she can read it for me.

"Juls," Beck says with his eyes still closed. I wince as I listen to Martina read, hardly able to hear him over her rising voice. "Please don't feed the wild animals."

"Shut it," Martina snaps at him, and goes back to reading. " 'Inventor breezed five furlongs in 1:01.64 on August 26. Celia Carter, who rode the colt in the Tremont, is also expected to make her first return to Saratoga in over four years.' "

Martina shuts the *Form* with such force I can hear the paper rip. She throws it down on the floorboards and kicks it with her shoe for added effect. There goes any hope I have of saving the article for posterity. I keep that thought to myself, because Martina is in no mood.

"Okay," I say slowly, taking stock of the atmosphere in the cab of the truck. It's somewhere around tense enough to snap or cut with a knife, whichever is more daunting. "I think we all have the information."

"So please don't delude yourself into believing she'll miss the plane, or lose the ride," Martina says. "Mom might be a complete space cadet, but there's no way she won't show up. The question is if she'll go on avoiding us as per usual."

"Okay, that's enough," Dad's roar is enough to shock all three of us into total silence. Beck shifts uncomfortably next to me on the backseat, probably envisioning leaping from a moving vehicle to get away from our family implosion. I wouldn't blame him at all if he did. At least we're turning onto the Blackbridge property, so this torture will be over soon enough.

Right when I think we might all be shocked to silence for the rest of the short drive to the barn, Martina proves me wrong. She stares right at Dad and says, "What's the likelihood that you knew about this?"

Dad's grip on the steering wheel tightens, and my knees start bouncing because I am that eager to claw my way out of this cab the second it lurches to a halt.

"Beck," Dad says, which is about the last thing I expected to hear, while he parks the rig outside of the barn. If Beck's stunned expression is any indication, he didn't expect to get singled out either. "I want you to get the hell out and go help Gus with your horse."

"Gladly," he says, shooting me a pitying look as he blindly searches for the handle of the back door on the twin cab. I watch him struggle with finding the handle and he partially falls, practically flies right out of the truck. The door slams behind him, and Lighter lets loose a whinny of pent up frustration.

Martina sits sideways in the front seat, her jaw set in the most self-righteous pose she can muster, our dad in her sights. I glance between them and wait for the other shoe to drop.

Finally Dad unbuckles his seat belt and says, "I want both of you up in the loft in five minutes."

With that he gets out of the truck, slams the door closed and stalks out of sight, probably to see if Lighter hasn't scratched himself up during his minor car trip tantrum.

Martina opens her mouth and then shuts it, turning away from me with this angry little grunt. Without a word to me, she opens the door and hops out of the cab. I'm finally left alone with an uncomfortable truth and my thoughts to keep me company. It occurs to me that I don't like that at all, and before I know it, I'm climbing out of the backseat, ready to face whatever chaos my family can throw at me.

~~

Here's the thing about Mom: I know she doesn't mean it. I know she didn't want to let us slip out of her fingers, but now we're gone and she's left with whatever she gave us up for—a personal mission and a Kentucky Derby winner she hasn't yet attained. What I don't know is if she regrets her decision, but maybe I'm thinking too much in terms of black and white.

I know that's Martina's mindset. It took her a while to come to this, somewhere between when Mom put off her first visit home for a horse and when everything went wrong with Matthew Delaney. I don't know if Martina thinks she has more to be pissed about, or if she's angry that she's here now to witness all of this when she could have easily been back in the safety of the city, ignoring it like she usually does.

When I walk into the loft, Martina is sitting at the table with her back to me. Her long dark hair is still in its messy ponytail, totally uncharacteristic of her usual suave poise, but since she's started working with us there's been less opportunity to keep up with personal style. Her shoulders are slumped, and it occurs to me that I am certainly not the one most affected by this news. I always assumed that Martina would never skip a beat the moment I found Mom's name in any one of those programs. Looks like I was wrong.

I pull out a chair across the table from her and sit down. She barely spares me a glance before Dad comes trooping in, walking into the kitchen and taking a minute to wash the barn off his hands. Stalling tactic, I think, but I keep my mouth shut while he turns off the tap and walks around the kitchen counter with a towel in his hands. He tosses it on the countertop and I sigh, wishing just once that someone would neatly fold something and at least try to be orderly.

This isn't the best time to bring that up, so I stay quiet, watching him come around Martina and take the third chair between us. He leans his forearms on the table.

"I am only going to say this once," he begins, clasping his hands together and giving us his parental authority voice. "What your mother does with her career is her business. I have always supported those decisions with the knowledge that whatever she did, I had the ways and means to take care of the both of you. I realize this situation was never ideal, to say the least."

Martina chews the inside of her cheeks with a vengeance, but she waits him out. So do I.

Dad lifts a hand to his hair and scrubs his fingers through it savagely, then says, "We're not perfect people."

Martina scoffs, and I nudge her leg hard with the toe of my boot.

"Highly imperfect," Dad says for Martina's benefit. "I'm sure there are plenty of things we could have done better, and we weren't very diligent about putting aside this life for anything else. Your mother is . . . motivated."

"Understatement of my life," Martina mutters.

"But," he says, looking at her, "she's also not under any obligation to ask me or us or you, Martina, if she's allowed to ride at Saratoga, Aqueduct, or Belmont for that matter."

I know I'm making a face that resembles all the bitterness I feel about that, but Martina lets it be known what she thinks.

"Bullshit," she says. "No one wants her to ask our permission, Dad. We want her to call and say she's going to be within a mile radius of us for at least twenty-four hours. How hard is that?" She looks at me. "Right? I'm not the only one thinking this, am I?"

"No," I say finally, shaking my head. "You're not."

"Then by all means," Dad says, shifting to pull his cell phone out of his pocket and tossing it onto the table, where it clatters to a halt in front of us, "call her. You both know her number."

Martina visibly winces and shrinks away from the table.

There's a moment's worth of awkward silence.

"I don't see why we should," I say quietly, my gaze lingering on the phone and then moving up to Martina, then Dad. "It's not exactly a two-way street, Dad. She went to California. She went everywhere that wasn't here. I get that it's her job, but it's never been about her not being here. It's about her not *trying* to be here."

I stand and snatch the phone up, handing it back to him. He takes it, surprised. "No one is blaming you," I say. "But calling? That's her responsibility, not ours."

Martina slumps back in her chair and I decide that I'm finished with this conversation. I slip past Dad's chair and leave the loft, thumping down the stairs and landing in the mess of the barn aisle.

The first thing I see is Kali, her head peeking around the opening of her stall. I can see her brown eyes catch sight of me, and she shifts closer to the door, turning her head to give me a curious look.

"Okay," I say to myself, taking a brief trip to the tack room to snag her bridle. When I get back to her stall, she's standing right there waiting for me.

Chapter Seventeen

I don't bother with a saddle. It's just one of those days. When I get the bridle on Kali, I lead her out of the stall and up to this ancient mounting block outside the barn. One hop and I get my belly over her back, then slide my leg over and straighten. It's not the most graceful move, and Kali is already prancing around in a decidedly confused circle by the time I get my legs around her and give her some direction.

We take off briskly for the galloping lanes, Kali's back rising and falling underneath me in her steady four-beat rhythm before I bounce my legs against her sides and she takes off into a rollicking canter.

I don't care where we go, or how we get there. I don't care about her form, or mine, or the fact that I'm breaking about every rule Dad's ever put in place about the galloping lanes. Kali's bareback, and I didn't bother with a helmet, which is infinitely stupid of me considering the fact that Kali's got enough youthful unpredictability to kill me if she really went crazy.

It's easy not to think about that. Kali keeps cantering and cantering, going up one rise and down another, rocking along. Her heat rises into my legs, but it's comfortable instead of sweltering. I think briefly of asking for more from her, but the thought slips away. Kali isn't a racer. Never was.

The galloping lanes are deserted, which is what I need. I slow Kali down to a walk and she obliges with a happy kick that threatens to send me on her neck unless I snag a fist in her mane. I settle back down in the dip of her back and let go. Eventually, we stop and I let her drop her head to the grass. I dismount and pull the reins over her head, then plop down on the ground next to her.

Kali lifts her head and nudges my knee, then buries her mouth back in the green grass with a blissful sigh of a horse that doesn't get enough of it. I watch her for a while, doing some mental calculations of my bank account in an effort to keep my mind off of the Hopeful. Delaney won't give her up for nothing, although she's virtually worthless as a racehorse and at best average in terms of bloodlines. Her babies would be wild cards, dependent on a good, expensive stallion to improve their quality.

A couple thousand would probably cut it. I've got a couple thousand. Now I need an opportunity, and maybe an injection of courage.

"Think you'd like a career change, girl?" I ask her, getting a mere ear flick in response as she rips mercilessly at a clump of clover I'm sitting on.

She'd be good with flat work, maybe even better over jumps. Time will tell, and she's young yet. It's a good thing I've got more than enough patience.

I hear hoofbeats that aren't Kali's and look over my shoulder, where Maggie's familiar splotches appear over the rise. I think maybe it's Dad, or maybe Beck, out searching for me, and I'm surprised to see Martina up on my mare's back. She pulls Maggie up when she sees me, and I wave her over.

Maggie bounces into a trot that's heavy on the forehand, her weight leaning on the reins. When Martina gets to me, she leaps off gracefully and unsnaps her helmet.

"That was stupid." She shoves the helmet in my hands.

"This is touching, Martina," I say, handing the helmet back to her, "but you need this more than I do."

She huffs, but takes it back.

"What are you doing out here?" I ask as she pulls Maggie's reins over the mare's head and lets her graze next to Kali. The two horses do nothing more then switch their tails at each other, content with the arrangement so long as there is grass. Martina folds her legs under her and settles on the ground next to me.

"'Well, it didn't seem to me that it was very fair that you got to run off without telling a soul," she shrugged. "So I went too."

I laugh. "Great. Dad will love that."

"No," she says. "But it's not really him, you know? It's not him at all."

"Mom." It's a statement I throw out there, and Martina looks down at her shoes. She's wearing a beaten up old pair of paddock boots I've got on loan to her. The heels are coming loose, and that must bug Martina to hell and back, but she accepted them without question. Something about better to take a crappy old pair for a week or two than it would be to buy a new pair she never wanted to begin with. So I wound up with a new pair of boots. Yay me.

"What's your plan?" she finally asks.

I dig at a patch of grass with the heel of my boot until it comes loose from the dirt. "I'm beginning to think I don't want to waste my time thinking about Mom."

"July," Martina rests her elbows on her knees, giving me a look I know well. "You've been scouring newsprint for months hunting for Mom's name. I thought you had dedicated a certain amount of time per day to Mom."

"Maybe I stopped thinking so much about it," I say, and I realize that I have. At some point, Saratoga stopped being about whether or not Mom would show up. "It feels like one more thing I can't change. Just like Blackbridge and Diver and maybe even Kali."

"Kali was always going to suck, July," Martina reminds me. "No extra time you put into her would have changed that."

"I know that," I say. "I wasn't exactly riding her to boost her stamina and speed."

A ghost of a smile appears on Martina's face and she nudges me in the arm. "Surreptitious behavior. Good for you, Juls."

"But I'm not doing that anymore," I say. "I'll man up and buy Kali."

"You'll buy Kali?" Martina asks, genuine surprise crossing her face. "Why?"

"Why not?" I ask in return. "She tries for me, just like Diver tried. She might not be a racehorse, but I'm not looking for . . ."

I stop suddenly, swallowing back a certain thickness in my throat at the thought of my big gray gelding. I shake my head, rubbing the back of my hand against my eyes. "I want her."

Martina stares up at the horses, and nods. "Then you should have her."

I let out a breath, and smile. I have no idea how I'm going to go about buying Kali, but at least I have Martina on my side.

"But what are you going to do about Mom?" Martina asks.

"You're right," I say. "Mom will be here. She won't pass up the opportunity at a good two-year-old. New York is an extended side trip for a horse like Inventor. He'll go to the Breeders' Cup Juvy, and he'll do the Santa Anita preps this spring, and we'll see him again in the Derby. It's all laid out for her if things go well."

Martina worries her bottom lip between her teeth for a minute and then says, "I can go home, you know."

I laugh. It bubbles up unexpectedly and bursts forth like I've actually got enthusiasm for this idea. "You'd avoid her altogether," I say, my voice accusing enough for her to wince slightly.

"I don't know," Martina says, shrugging. "Maybe."

"You'd leave her to me," I say. "Just like last time. Thanks a lot, Martina. That's very sisterly of you."

"Wait," she holds her hands up and repeats the phrase while I'm busy getting up. She grabs my wrist and hauls me back down into the grass. "Damn it, July. Wait. I wasn't at Aqueduct that day because I just wasn't. Had I been there, I would have avoided her like you did."

I pull my wrist out of her grip and say, "Yeah, but that's the thing. I didn't avoid her. I tried to talk to her, and I never got the chance."

"What?"

"I didn't ignore the fact that she was there, Martina," I say as clearly as I can. "I only found out that she was riding that day, and by the time I realized I didn't want to avoid her, it was way too late. She was gone."

She doesn't say anything. Instead she shakes her head and watches the horses. Right about now I could do without her sudden urge to be introspective. I want to fill the silence with as many words as I can find.

"That's why I keep checking the programs and the news, so I know what days to go to the track," I say. "It's worked out so far because her name hasn't shown up. Now, however, she's in the damned Hopeful, and I'm not going to let her run me away from that race."

I must have said it with enough conviction for Martina to take me seriously. "You're going to go to the Hopeful?"

"Yes," I say. "Lighter is running. It's our last summer here with Blackbridge, and I'm not going to let Mom of all people screw that up for me."

"Do you know what you'll say to her?" she asks. "I can't imagine she can avoid conversation if you're right there in the paddock with her."

"I don't know," I say, because I'm genuinely clueless on that part. I know that I can't sit out the Hopeful because my mom is riding for the competition.

"Well," Martina says after a second, and then lapses into another silence so deep I can hear the horses munching on their grass. Finally she says, "I guess I can witness that."

"You guess?"

She rolls one shoulder and bobs her head in a nod. "Sure. Besides, I can't let you get all the glory."

I stand up and offer her my hand. She takes it and hauls herself out of the grass. "You really think this is a good idea?"

She puts on her helmet, and buckles it underneath her chin. "Good as it can get, I guess."

I nod and gather up Kali's reins. The filly lifts her head from the grass while I ask Martina for a leg up. She puts a hand on my shin and lifts while I hop, doing my awkward maneuvering over Kali's back. When I'm situated, she goes to Maggie and mounts up.

For a minute, we stand there, looking at each other from the backs of the horses. If someone told me I'd see my sister on a horse again, I'd have fallen over laughing.

"Hey," I say to her. "Why did you quit?"

"I decided I didn't need to share anything else with Mom. Why do you keep doing it?"

That's a good question. The hours suck, the pay is almost nonexistent, the chance of serious injury is through the roof, but I shrug because I've only got one answer. "I love it."

She laughs. "I guess we're Mom's horse girls."

Two sides of the same coin. Wouldn't Mom be proud?

❧

The rest of the day is a wash. We all go our separate ways, as if we've had far too much family time from the short moments we spent on Mom.

I can't imagine what the rest of the week is going to be like. I can't imagine what I should imagine it to be like. The concept is totally foreign to me, this looming truth that Celia Carter will be riding in the Hopeful, and that I will be there, right there, to see it. I'll be in touching distance, speaking distance, and right now I don't have any words.

What do you say? There might be something to that whole avoidance solution after all.

I'm curled up on the sofa watching late night television, unable to sleep, when something taps against the screen of the open window. I think it must be a disoriented bug, distracted by the glow from the television, until I hear a ping against the glass. I right myself on the sofa and crawl over to the window, staring into the darkness.

Beck is down there, tossing a handful of gravel onto the parking lot.

"What are you doing?" I ask him through the screen, resting my arms against the windowsill.

"Seeing who was awake," he says, rubbing the gravel dust on his jeans. I squint down at him. He's totally cocooned in the dark, the barn lights distorting his shadow into a long slice behind his feet.

"It never occurred to you that it might not be me?"

I can see his grin in the stark relief of the light. "Who else would it be?"

He knows my family too well, but today is one of those off days. "After this morning, chances are it could have been anyone."

"Yeah," he says, peering up at me. "How was that?"

"I'd say it bore some similarities to experiencing a dysfunctional war room," I say, pressing the side of my head against the window and leaning my elbows into the back of the sofa.

"So what's the verdict?" he asks, and unease settles into my stomach. I glance behind me at the closed bedroom doors. The lights are off, but I'd rather not do this all Romeo and Juliet style.

"I'm coming down," I tell him, pushing from the windowsill and hardly catching Beck's belated, "Uh, okay?" because I'm already padding into my bedroom and digging for something to wear. I come up with cut offs to replace the worn old sleep shorts, because it's too hot for jeans. I toe into my pair of flip-flops and make my way out of the loft, squeaking down the old wooden stairs.

I find Beck sitting on the trunk of my car. He's kicked his shoes off and rests his bare feet on my bumper. I abandon my foam flip-flops and join him, hopping up onto the warm metal.

We sit there for a minute, cicadas screaming in the trees and the nearly clear night sky spinning stars over our heads. He doesn't repeat his question. In fact, he rests against the back window of my car and puts his arms behind his head. I realize the ball must be in my court again, so I lean back against the window next to him and fold my legs up on the trunk.

"Sorry about that scene in the truck," I start, and he makes a noncommittal noise. "It was the initial freak out, so none of us were being normal."

"The great Celia Carter returns to New York," he says. "Whoever saw that coming?"

Me? I bite my lip.

"It wasn't unexpected," I say. "When this sort of thing happens, she tends to drop out of the middle of nowhere and then disappears again."

Despite the heat, I fold my arms across my stomach, tucking my fingers against the car. I can feel Beck watching me, so I turn to face him.

"When was she here last?" is what he asks me.

"February," I say. "The Whirlaway Stakes."

A sound of disbelief catches in his throat, and he shakes his head, looks away for a minute.

"She turned up at Aqueduct for about a split second and disappeared again," I say. "I missed her, or she was very good at eluding me. Maybe she didn't realize I was even there."

"Bullshit, Juls," Beck says, ripping what little assurance that hypothetical might have away from me. "Where else would you have been?"

"My mom," I say, pausing to try to explain this. It's not like she's normal. She's a horse girl. She's exactly like me. My stomach clenches at the thought. "She's been following a dream for a very long time."

Beck smiles at that, one of his methodical, wry smiles. "She's been gone for a very long time, you mean."

"I'm not trying to justify her actions," I say.

"It sounds like you are."

"Well, I'm not."

"I'm glad you cleared that up," Beck says.

I smack my knuckles lightly against his knee, but he grabs my hand, tangles our fingers together and keeps me trapped there. Trying to pull out of his grip doesn't work with Beck, so I turn onto my side and poke him in the ribs with my free hand. That eventually doesn't work either, because Beck is nothing if not industrious. I wind up with both hands trapped in his, a victorious Beck giving me a devious look from the other side of my car.

We're already pretty close, but he pulls me closer. His nose brushes against mine when I say, "I am going to the Hopeful."

His head tips back, regards me with a perplexed glint. "I'm glad?"

"Just in case, you know, you thought that I wouldn't."

"Honestly, July," he says, "I never assumed you wouldn't be there."

"Because I've been so supportive of Lighter since you bought him," I say, resting my hands against his shirt. It's black this time around, with the word *Atheist* written on it in big block letters. I pluck at it aimlessly. He shifts closer, the corner of his mouth lifting up.

"Sure you have," he says. "After he proved that you were completely wrong and he actually has talent. Also, he is the only horse at Blackbridge that will be trained under Carter Racing Stables in a few months. There is that."

I make a sour face, poking a finger against his chest. "You just had to bring that up, didn't you?"

"Sure I did."

"Carter Racing Stables?" I ask.

"Do you expect your dad to be more creative? Besides, since Lighter is currently without a jockey, I'd say Rob has more things to worry about than his future stable name."

I sober up, and pull out of his grip, rolling onto my back. The car is hard and uncomfortable underneath me, so I sit up. Beck's eyes are on the back of my neck.

"I thought Jorge was riding for us in the Hopeful," I say, but Beck shakes his head.

"He committed elsewhere before Pilar broke her arm," he says. "Your dad is pulling strings."

"I'll bet," I say, trying to let Beck's easy attitude rub off on me. He's not worried, so I shouldn't be worried, right? It's his horse and Dad is the best around at picking a jockey.

I take a deep, steadying breath and will myself to let it float away.

"What are you going to say to her?" Beck asks my back, and I push my hair out of my face, looking at him over my shoulder.

"That's kind of the part of the plan that's eluding me," I say. "After showing up, it gets unscripted."

"What would you have told her at the Whirlaway?" he asks. "If you'd met up with her?"

I laugh, tipping my head back and closing my eyes. "I probably would have grabbed her," I say. "I would have grabbed her and asked her . . ."

That's where it gets sticky. Truthfully, I don't know what I would have asked her. Deep down, I have a feeling it would have been about her. How is she? Is she coming back? *Why the hell did she leave us?* None of that feels right now, because we all know the answers to the most important of those questions. She's not coming back. The rest of it is small talk.

Why the hell did she leave? There's no answer to that one. Any attempt would be a shitty excuse.

"I would have asked her something inconsequential," I say. "Everything is different now."

Beck tugs on one of the belt loops of my frayed shorts, and I make myself meet his eyes.

"Nothing you have to tell or ask her is inconsequential," he says. "You know that."

"I do," I say. "But all of that? I don't really care about it anymore."

"Okay," he says, sits up. My eyes travel automatically up to his face; he frames mine in his hands. "So what are you going to tell her? What do you want to tell her?"

I pause, and dig my nails against the metal. What do I want to tell my mother? What needs to be said?

"I'll say . . ." I lick my lips. "I'll say good luck. Break a leg."

Beck grins, moves his fingers down to trace over my jaw and settle on my neck. "She's got no hope, you know."

Before I can say anything to that, he leans forward and kisses me.

I kiss him right back.

Chapter Eighteen

The grandstand rumbles under my feet, the track bursting with noise and popping camera flashes as I stand in the winner's circle watching Galaxy Collision approach to the applause of thirty thousand.

Somewhere the announcer booms, "Returning to the winner's circle is Galaxy Collision!"

The Woodward Stakes is in the books, and Galaxy Collision is the winner by the tip of her nose. The filly is unbreakable and still undefeated. Her hooves clop unevenly on the brick, veins raised underneath her sweat-stained coat and dark brown eyes ringed with white. Adrenaline still pumps through her as Jorge shouts victorious words at the receptive crowd, Izzie finding room for the filly amongst every Blackbridge employee who wants in the photograph.

The smiles on our faces are enough for tears to spike at the back of my eyes, just as Martina wraps me in a bear hug and whispers, "Don't you dare start crying. Today is a happy day."

I laugh, because I hope it will only get better. In a few moments, I'm going to try to ride this phenomenal high and ask Delaney if I can buy Kali. Beck has assured me that if I catch him with his guard down, wallowing in the excess glee that comes when your wonder filly completely destroys the Woodward Stakes, that I'll have my best shot. So I'm going to take it.

The photographer picks that moment to capture us clustered together next to the filly that couldn't lose. Jorge jumps off Gal's back to another whoop from the crowd, stopping on his way back to the jock's room to sign racing programs that are thrust in his direction over the fence. Galaxy is led back to the barns, dripping from her cool down soak and swinging her rump from side to side.

"When are you going to ask Mr. Delaney?" Martina asks me under her breath as we walk with the flow into the grandstand. Our considerable party is giddy, floating on winning a $750,000 purse and throwing propriety to the wind. Olivia Delaney bops along in front of me, waving to onlookers who wolf whistle her way.

"Well?" Martina asks, prompting Beck's curiosity.

"What are you two whispering about?"

Martina shushes him, and he throws up his hands. "Fine. Who am I to understand sisterly bonding?"

"Go bond with Matt," Martina says, waving him away. "Maybe you can convince him to stop asking me out to lunch."

"The man just wants a little closure, Martina," Beck says, and Martina laughs like that's the last thing she needs, pushing him in Matt's direction.

"I'll do it as soon as Dad goes back to the barns," I whisper to Martina, stepping into the cool air conditioning of the Saratoga Room, where the bar is already lined with champagne flutes filled with bubbling, beckoning liquid.

"And when does he typically do that?"

"Earlier than you'd think," I say, stopping amidst the tables and grabbing Martina's hand. "If he doesn't go in the next thirty minutes, find a way to distract him away from Delaney."

"I don't get why this has to be such a secret," Martina says, squeezing my hand all the same. Sister solidarity.

"Because I didn't run it by him first."

I wince when Martina's face contorts into a series of disbelieving expressions, finally settling on exasperation. "What? July, that is completely . . ."

"I know," I hiss, shaking my head. "I know, I really know. It's just something I need to do, and I don't want his help."

"Oh, you think he'll help, huh?" Martina laughs. "Good luck when you give him the news."

"Yeah, yeah," I sigh, perking up when Beck approaches with three flutes snagged from the bar.

"Ladies?" He hands two over to us, and my shaky fingers wrap around the delicate glass thankfully.

"I didn't know I was old enough for this," I tell him, while Martina tips hers back in a dainty sip.

"You aren't," he tells me. "But neither am I, for that matter. It's just that I get special treatment. Who can say no to me?"

"Plenty of people," Martina says, deadpan.

"You're welcome," Beck smiles back.

I take a tiny sip of the champagne, dry bubbles bursting on my tongue and sliding on a slippery path down my throat. Some of the tension begins to ease away, and I take a thorough look around the room, noticing who has clustered at the bar and the smattering of tables. My father is laughing with Delaney, clinking champagne flutes while race reporters shout out toasts to big wins at the betting windows.

For a room dedicated to winning big, it's remarkably simple. My offer to buy Kali should be equally simple. Simple enough plan, simple enough offer. Dampness forms at the small of my back, proof positive that my heart is racing as I wait. Nothing is ever as simple as it seems.

Before I can instruct Martina to lure Dad away, he finishes his champagne and slaps Delaney on the back—the manly show of congratulations—and turns to find all three of us holding our illegal beverages.

He raises an eyebrow.

"It was forced on me," Beck hastily explains.

"Good," Dad says in return, walking past our surprised faces to the door. "You all deserve it. I'll be getting things ready to go at the barn. Juls, I'll need you sooner rather than later."

"Understood," I nod, looking down at my drink to keep him from seeing my nervous trembling.

Martina makes a show of rolling her eyes once Dad has left the Saratoga Room. "It's not like the man can't know."

"It would make for exceedingly less drama later," Beck says under his breath, as if I can't hear him.

"It's not about Dad," I say, shrugging back my shoulders. It's time to do this. "It's about Kali."

I hand my champagne glass over to Martina and spin around, honing in on my target. It takes all of five steps before I arrive at the bar, my target acquired. Delaney smiles over at me, a new flute of champagne bubbling up in his fingers. I smile shakily back.

"Congratulations." A wide smile blooms over his perfectly white teeth, and he pats me on the back like he would Dad. The force of it pushes me closer to the bar.

"No," he says. "That mare is all your dad. He saw her, bought her, and trained her. I just handed him the cash."

"That's . . ." I pause, cocking my head at him. "Remarkably correct."

He laughs, putting the glass down on the bar. "I'm going to miss this," he tells me. "It's not every day you get to experience a horse like that."

"Most people don't," I nod. "We were lucky."

"I'll drink to that," he says, taking a healthy swallow.

"I wanted to ask you a question," I say, deciding it's time to jump in.

"Sure," he says, so easily I feel like I'm falling into a trap. That's ridiculous, so I continue.

"You don't want Kali."

"Which one is Kali?" he asks. Like father, like son.

"Kaliningrad. You don't want her."

That's a statement, and he tips his head at me curiously. "I don't?"

"No," I say. "You've put her in so many claimers over the past few months, and she's routinely done so horribly in them that it would be wise of you to cut her loose."

"Okay," he nods. "I would say that's a correct assessment."

"Then I'd like to offer to buy her," I say, all the while wondering if I'm completely screwing this up. I've been to auctions, I've seen horses sold privately, but I've never done it myself. There are nuances I'm not sure I'll ever learn, but I'm not sure if Delaney knows that or not. He doesn't look surprised by my offer, that's for sure.

"She could be a worthwhile investment as a broodmare," he points out to me.

"Mr. Delaney," I say, "the facts are that you're selling Blackbridge, and logically that means the breeding end of the farm will go first. Kali could be a broodmare, but given that we can't convince anyone to claim her, I can't see how she'd bring a lot of value into an auction ring. Her bloodlines aren't anything extraordinary, and her sire was recently sold to a farm in Texas. You'd be wasting money getting someone to bid on her."

The corner of his mouth quirks up, and he smiles. "I take it you've given this some thought."

"Of course," I say. "She raced for a twenty grand tag and didn't sell. You haven't lowered it much further than that because I know you want some assurance that she'll go to a good home."

He doesn't say anything to that. True, I might be stretching it. I'm not sure whether or not he cares where she goes. I'm going to assume he's got her best interests at heart, because at least it gives me something to work with.

"The fact is I can provide her a good home. Just for a bit less."

"How much less are we talking about, July?"

I swallow down a frog in my throat.

"Two thousand."

Delaney smiles, and calls the bartender over for a napkin. She brings one over, the little white square sitting between us on the shiny wood.

"How about this," Delaney says, bringing a heavy pen out of his suit pocket and writing across the napkin in thick, black ink. "You sign to this agreement, transfer the agreed upon amount, and we have a deal."

"What is it that I'm signing?" I ask, the words dying in my throat when he pushes the napkin over to me.

I, Lawrence Delaney, sell the filly Kaliningrad to July Carter for the price of $1.

Underneath is his scribbled name.

"I offered two thousand," I say, my voice squeaking.

"And I'm offering you a better deal," he says. "I think you should take it."

I swallow, looking up at him. "Why?"

He purses his lips, as if he hadn't expected to explain himself. Then he laughs and says, "Because you've been with us forever, Juls. You're right about the filly, and I think you'd provide her a better home than she could get on the track. And I had a great damn day. Take the offer."

I laugh, picking up the napkin and his pen. "Of course I'm taking the offer."

I sign my name to the delicate paper, the tip of the pen catching on the fiber and blotting ink on the tips of my fingers. I don't care, though. I'm so far past caring as I open up my clutch, thumb past the blank check I had waiting, and pull out one of the singles stashed there instead.

He accepts the bill, folding it in half and sliding it without ceremony into his pocket.

"I'll have the paperwork drawn up tomorrow," he says, and then lifts a glass out of the waiting rows of champagne, handing it to me.

"To Kaliningrad," he says, clinking his glass with mine. Warmth spreads through my chest, weaves around my ribs and settles somewhere deep inside. Kali is mine. *Mine, mine, mine.* There will never be any letting her go.

"To Kaliningrad," I echo, and drink.

Martina's happy shriek can be heard around the room, not that many people even notice. There's too much drinking and laughing to notice our behavior. I hop up and down with her, clutching the napkin between us.

"A napkin?" Beck asks, taking it from me and shaking his head as he studies it. "That's so unlike him."

"Maybe he doesn't like you as much as he likes me," I say, plucking it back and squirreling it into my clutch.

"That's fair," Beck says, drawing me up to him and bending down enough for a quick kiss. I smile against his lips, and Martina makes a mock disgusted grunt.

"I'm getting another glass of champagne," she announces, spinning around. "Try to be done making out when I return."

"I make no promises," Beck calls after her, and she gives him the finger as she disappears into the crowd. I laugh, hiding my smile behind my hands until he draws them away and says, "Congratulations. I know you wanted her."

"I did," I nod. "I do. Now the hardest part is telling Dad."

"He'll love it," Beck says, dismissing my concern with a wave of his hand. I raise an eyebrow. "Deep down, anyway. Deep down he'll be thrilled."

"Right," I nod once, and take a deep breath. "Speaking of which, I should probably go tell him about it now that it's done."

"Want any back up?" Beck asks, downing the rest of his glass and shoving his hands in his pockets, tipping forward on his toes in anticipation.

"Absolutely." I take his hand and tug him toward the door, as another flow of visitors walks through the door to shouts and applause.

It's Jorge. Of course, it's Jorge. He's freshly showered, black hair slicked back, a smile stretching over his face as he leads a contingent of fawning followers in bright, flowing dresses. I cast a knowing look at Beck, and we trade glances. When I turn back, expecting to shout out at Jorge that he couldn't be any more predictable, someone else catches my eye.

Beck catches my wrist, so I know. He's seen her, too.

The breath in my lungs slowly drains out of my mouth, and I fail to pull more in. For a moment I am so still I can feel my heart pumping, the echo pounding in my ears. It only starts to go faster, beginning to race as I gasp for air.

"July," Beck says softly as my eyes start to water. "July?"

Everything in front of me is a haze, but I can see her. I can see her clear as day.

My mother stands, half in and half out of the Saratoga Room. Her long, yellow dress trails around her feet, far too long for her, but acting like a beacon in a sea of celebration. Trepidation is written all over her face, and I'm glad for a moment that she knows that she has no right to be here.

But then Celia Carter wasn't the best with social niceties, because when she locks eyes on me she half-heartedly smiles and takes that extra step inside when she should be turning around and walking away. She walks right up to me, her sandaled feet silent on the floor and her fingers wringing together because she knows how this is going to go.

We both know. Even Beck knows. And still I stand here like a statue, unwilling to move.

She stops in front of me, and through the sound of my heartbeat I hear her say, "It's nice to see you, July."

My mouth is pinched shut, heat raging through my veins and along my skin. Beck is a comforting weight at my back, his hand still on my wrist, thumb moving in a distracting circle on my thready pulse. I don't know where Martina is, but I can feel her eyes on us from across the room and I quietly hope she'll stay away.

Mom shifts her weight, waiting for me to say something, her cocoa brown eyes dancing from my face to Beck to our feet and back. All I can really think to say is *how dare you come here? How dare you even think it?*

But I don't want to waste my breath.

"Mom," I say, letting the word hang there between us.

She lets out a breath, like she's been waiting for a sign that everything is okay and this is it. She can rest easy now that I've acknowledged her.

"Jorge found me," she says, beginning to rattle on. "I couldn't say no, of course. You know how he is, and I thought I might as well, seeing as how the Hopeful has turned out."

"How the Hopeful has turned out?" I echo, so aware of the people around me that my confusion over her statement is painful.

"Sure," Mom says, hugging herself now, as though she's unsure about plunging on, which she does regardless. "Now that I'm riding for Blackbridge."

The words hit me like arrows, piercing so deeply that I have to take a step back, shrinking away.

"No," is all I can think to say, shaking my head. I shrink further back as my mother reaches for me. I pull out of Beck's grasp so I can keep her from touching me. "That's . . . no."

"I made the commitment this morning," Mom says softly, her hands dropping to her sides.

What do you say to that? I swing to Beck, looking for confirmation. He only shrugs, as stunned as I am.

"I have to go," I say, darting around her, focused entirely on the door.

"Juls," Mom starts, but I cut her off.

"Don't," I snarl at her. "I don't want to hear it."

With that I'm off, shoving my way through the door and weaving through the crowds until the bodies part and I can break into a run. It doesn't take long to arrive at the backside, the crunch of gravel under my flats insisting I bring my harried pace down to a brisk walk. I'm breathing hard when I appear in our shedrow, my face streaming with tears I wasn't aware I'd shed.

Dad is in the aisle, talking with Galaxy's groom as the filly stands impatiently between them. Sensing my arrival, they both look up, and the glitter of post-race excitement dies out of Dad's eyes.

"You saw her," he says, and I stiffen.

"Of course I did," I say. "How could I miss her when she walked right into the Saratoga Room? I would have been awed by the gall, if not for the fact that she's riding Lamplighter in the Hopeful."

Dad nods, pressing his mouth into a firm line.

"Is that all, or should I brace myself for more?" I ask, walking around Galaxy's hindquarters and stopping a horse length away, crossing my arms across my chest and squeezing them tight. "Are you finally getting divorced? Or, God, are you getting back together? She's not moving back in, is she? Because I'm having a hard time figuring out how that would work given the fact that she's been gone for *four years*."

My voice has picked up several notices, hitting shrill. I'm shaking and unable to stop, even when Dad comes around Galaxy and pulls me into a hug. My stilted breathing is muffled by his shirt, coming in and out in ragged pants.

"No," he says. "No, of course not. It's just a race, Juls."

"And out of all the jockeys on the East Coast, you pick her," I say, closing my eyes because the afternoon light is slanting into the barn and glinting in my tears.

"She fits a certain set of parameters," he says. "That's all."

"Did one of those parameters take into account driving Martina and I crazy?" I ask, pulling myself away. He looks at me pityingly, and I want to snap at him that Mom left him, too. Why was he always so calm about it? Why couldn't he ever tell her where to shove it?

"I can only consider what will give Lamplighter the best edge," he tells me, and I laugh.

Of course. The horses come first. This time, I don't want to understand.

"Do you even hear yourself?" I ask, pushing back. "She left us. She left *you*. You're giving her an opportunity she doesn't even deserve, and you're expecting us to be okay with it because she meets your *parameters*. How can you be okay?"

I don't realize that I'm screaming. I am causing a scene. I don't care.

Martina's sharp heeled shoes strike the concrete outside, and I heave a breath. Beck is with her, and when I turn around I see what I expect. Beck is awash in concern, hair a mess, and tie still resting over his shoulder from running. Martina holds herself straight as a pole and comes straight for me, wrapping me into a hug so tight I wonder which one of us is more wrecked.

"She's riding for us," I whisper to her.

"I know," is all she says, and hugs me tighter.

Chapter Nineteen

The training track at Saratoga is filled with horses spouting misty breath. They glisten red as the sun climbs up the trees, bathing warmth over my face in efforts to chase away the morning chill. I hunker down in my jacket, hands shoved in my pockets as I stand like a monolith along the outer rail.

"You really don't need to be here," Pilar says to my right, not looking at me. We're both too busy watching Lighter out on the track. My mom is riding him, her bright pink protective vest making them all the more obvious.

"Neither do you," I point out, and she smiles grimly, ducking her head.

"Well, maybe I need the closure."

I glance down at her cast and shake my head. "You'll be back on a horse in no time flat."

"You're right," she says, but then gestures at the track in front of us. "I just didn't expect this."

I snort. "No. This is all kinds of unexpected."

"Well," Pilar shrugs. "At least you got to see her this time."

I nod, because that's true. I did see her. Celia Carter has been seen and words have been exchanged, however charged. It's far better than trying and failing and having to live with it after.

Mom and Lighter come down from their easy gallop, just enough to get acquainted. The colt tosses his head, ducks toward the inside rail, and Mom straightens him out and keeps going like it's nothing. I frown at them as they transition down in front of us, cantering until they drop to a trot and then a walk, cooling off in a ramble on their way back up to us.

Dad is standing further down the rail. We haven't spoken. I haven't particularly felt the need, but I'm still drawn to the works like a moth to flame. Some part of me needs to figure this out, but right now I just stand here with my heart in my throat.

Dad's assistant taps numbers and notes into a tablet when my mom approaches them. Lighter jigs under her, snorting steaming breaths like a copper dragon and flicking his ears all about like he still can't come to grips with this human on top of him.

Mom and Dad speak all of a few words and then Dad jerks his head to the barns. My mom nods curtly, dismissed. I think they must act so professional to cover up the ocean of hurt underneath, but then what do I know? They're both so good at making our lives secondary that I would never know what bothers them outside of what filly has a strained tendon and what colt is off his feed. Their daughters must be so mystifying to them, with our demands for attention.

Lighter side step dances toward the gap in the rail, where Gus waits to snag him and lead him off to the shedrow. Mom lands gracefully on her feet, pats the colt absently on the shoulder, and pulls off her helmet to reveal all that glossy dark hair spilling underneath a blue bandana.

For a second she looks lost, unsure what to do in the gap. Dad has his back turned on her, speaking with the assistant. I turn my focus on the gravel between my toes, rooting myself to my spot no matter how hard Pilar bumps her hip against mine.

"Well?" she hisses. "Go on."

"No interest," I tell her, fully aware that I'm lying through my teeth. She bumps me again.

"Then why are you here?"

I open my mouth and snap it shut. Pilar smiles, but it dies at the crunch of gravel.

"Juls?"

I suck up a breath.

"Hey, Mom."

I can see her relief out of the corner of my eye, her shoulders settling and a breath slowly escaping her clenched lungs. I am still bottled up, hard to the touch, but if she notices she doesn't say anything. Instead she looks past me to Pilar.

"I'm sorry about your arm. This was your ride."

Pilar shrugs diplomatically. "I'll be back in no time," she says and I smile to myself as she pats my back with her good arm. Of course, Lighter is her ride. "I should get going. Nice to see you back, Celia."

We're quiet for a few moments, watching horses arrive and work and disappear back up to the barn. I can't help but think of a stalemate, only ours is where one person refuses to speak and the other doesn't know what to say.

Finally, she says, "I understand you've been riding in the mornings."

"I'm working for Dad," I tell her simply, only to the point and not much more.

"And that Martina . . ."

"She's working for Dad, too," I interrupt, getting irritated. Is this what we're going to waste our time talking about?

"Look," I push away from the rail. "I'll be needed back at the farm. You looked good on Lighter, so keep it up tomorrow at the race, okay? He means a lot to us."

"July," she says, jumping forward to grab my wrist as I try to flee. I yank away, getting Dad's attention from down the rail. His face looks stormy, like he's ready to do something I never anticipated and rescue me. I raise my fingers, asking him to stay put.

"What, Mom?"

"I was just hoping that . . ."

"That what?" I ask, knowing my voice is full of venom and letting it seep out anyway.

She presses. "I wanted to talk."

"About?"

"Everything," she shrugs. "I've missed out on a lot."

"Precisely everything," I tell her. "That's a pretty impossible task."

"I'm trying, July," she says, furrowing her eyebrows like she can't understand why I keep resisting when she's pushing so hard.

"All of a sudden," I mutter, shaking my head. "You can't just do this, okay? You can't blow in here and expect all of us to want the same things you want. It doesn't work that way."

She winces and looks down at her hands.

"I know," she nods. "It's a lot to ask, but I want to try to explain myself. And I want to ask if you'll listen."

My first thought is *no. No, I don't want to listen.* During the Whirlaway I would have jumped at the opportunity. I ran headlong into it, wanting it so much that I couldn't see anything past it. Then it slipped away. Mom slipped away.

But now I'm here, flittering around where I knew she would be, sabotaging my own attempts to not listen. I came here for a reason, so I would have to follow through. Backing out would just be running away, pulling a page out of Mom's book.

"You can buy me coffee," I say, so suddenly it surprises us both. Mom is quick to recover, a smile stretching over her lips.

"Absolutely," she nods, and leads the way to the track cafeteria.

I hang back for a second and turn back to catch Dad's eye. It's not hard, since he's watching like a hawk.

I silently mouth, "Coffee."

He nods and goes back to the works. I spin around and troop after Mom.

∿

The paper coffee cup sits between my feet on the bleachers, and Mom is talking. Her hands are flurries in the air, signing made up movements to her words, and I listen about the horses and the races that she can't stop describing even though I know them all by heart.

"I saw them." I finally interrupt her story. She blinks, as though shaking herself out of a reverie.

"I read about them, and I saw every race streaming online," I tell her. "I followed you for years up until this summer, because it was the only way I'd ever know what you were doing."

She's silent for a moment, and I hope that she's a little ashamed for taking up my time with racing stories.

"If this is all you have to tell me about," I say, picking up the coffee cup, "then I've got better things to do."

"No, wait," she says, shaking her head. "You're right. Of course you know all about the horses."

"Of course I do, Mom."

"I guess I'm blowing this," she sighs.

"Don't start," I say, standing up. "You wanted to talk to me, and I'm giving you that chance. Don't try to make me feel sorry for you because you can't come up with a good excuse for your absence."

"I'm just not good at this."

"I know that," I tell her. "But it's not my job to help you out."

"Okay," she says, patting the bleachers. "Please sit down, July."

I lower myself slowly, perching on the edge of the seat and cursing my own curiosity. My coffee is halfway gone and I've only silently listened to her West Coast success story, as if that's supposed to make me forgive her for all the mistakes she's carefully editing out. Martina would be gone by now, walking away with her hackles up. But I'm the queen of second chances, giving Mom more than her fair share.

"I think I'm afraid you won't forgive me," she says, looking down at her hands.

"That's not what this is about," I tell her carefully, and I know that hits her hard in the way she flinches. It's only then that I realize I've taken forgiveness off the table.

"Okay," she says again. "Okay. When I left for the California tracks that first year, it was always going to be temporary. I had all the reason in the world to come back, of course. I loved your father, loved you girls, loved a business that was doing better than I could have imagined. California really came out of left field, and I hadn't intended to go until your father encouraged me. It was the pinnacle of a jockey's career, after all. We decided that I should try for it. That I owed it to myself."

"And were never seen again," I say, huffing.

"Don't," Mom says, surprising me by snapping. "This was hard for me, July. Leaving and coming back was always the plan, but I was sidetracked by the challenge of it. It became more than testing out how I'd do over the season, and more about competing with the best the world had to offer me and I couldn't say no. God help me, I wanted to. I just couldn't."

I stare at her, words failing to appear to tell her how ridiculous she sounds.

"We planned trips for you girls to come visit," she continued. "But they fell through in the beginning and then . . . I'm ashamed to say that it became too hard."

"That's bullshit, you know." The words come out of my clenched teeth.

"I know," she nods.

"What about the Whirlaway? You were in New York and you deliberately ignored us."

"I know you were at the Whirlaway," she says, and I give her a look that must have appeared murderous for how quickly she added, "after the fact. Your father wouldn't let me hear the end of that for days."

"Good," I say. "What is wrong with you? You could have visited. You were right there."

"And say what?" she argues right back. "I couldn't just appear unannounced after so long. There was just . . . too much silence to cut through at that point. I'd let things go, got too caught up in the horses."

The eye roll I give her must be pretty dramatic, because she stops talking.

"I think I can say with definite certainty that some things are more important than the horses, Mom."

"I know," she says quietly. "I'm guilty of not realizing that initially, and then it just became too hard to pretend."

"How could you?" I ask finally, the words out there in the gulf between us now.

She shakes her head. "I don't know. I love you, but I failed you at the same time. I just hope I can salvage something of our family when I have the chance."

"Would you have done this had you not come for the Hopeful?" I ask, standing up because my body won't let me sit anymore. I'm too nervous to stay still.

She looks up at me and says carefully, "I knew the Hopeful was the right way to approach you. It was natural because of . . ."

"The horses," I finish for her.

"Pilar's arm and Lighter," she continues without correcting me, "made things easier."

"I don't want to keep doing this with you," I say to her. "I don't want to be a second thought to whatever horse you're offered."

"I don't want that either," she tells me genuinely, standing up. "I want to try to fix things."

"I don't know if you can," I tell her softly, taking a step back.

"But will you let me try?"

I pause, wondering what Martina would say. *No, no, no, leave us alone. We've come this far without you.* I don't want to hide behind steel walls and I don't want to be disappointed again. Where is the middle ground?

"I can't stop you from trying," is what I say, because that is true. I cannot stop her, and I only ever wanted her to reach for me. Maybe this is a good place to start. Her trying, and my expecting nothing. I can't be hurt, then, if I never expect her to follow through.

She nods, sharply, like she's been given a command.

"Just make sure you do right by Lighter," I tell her, and feel the irony rising up in my face. Of course, it's a horse that comes first.

"I'll steer him home safe," she says. It's a promise and she will follow through.

"Good," I say, and turn around, heading down the bleachers.

"See you tomorrow, July!" she calls after me. I wave to let her know I heard her, and shake my head as I go.

My whole life has been horses, and although I rail against my parents for always letting them run our lives I know I'm no better. How can I be? I've chosen them over Bri, over college, over a normal teenage existence.

Everything has always been about the horses, even now, when I have Mom right there in front of me. I'm so mad at her for all the right reasons, and all I really want of her is to ride Lighter well, to guide him home. My mother, the person, can wait.

Pot, meet Kettle.

The door opens with a whoosh, and Martina stands there in shorts, her long hair soaking into her cotton tank top.

"What was that?" she asks, putting her hands on her hips.

"It's always the horses with her," I shrug. "You know that."

She snorts, walking into the kitchen and pouring a glass of water. It is muggy in the apartment, a dull breeze creeping in through the windows doing little more than move the air around. "I don't accept that."

"No," I say. "Neither do I."

We trade glances. I know what she's thinking. That I might forgive her simply because I'm a horse girl, so caught up in this world that I'm guilty of pushing everything else to the periphery. I know I've done it, and I know that Martina thinks I've pushed her away, too.

She's right; I have.

She finally nods. "Good. That's good, July."

"So are you going to come to the race tomorrow?" I watch her put the glass down, circle it in the condensation it makes on the counter.

"I don't want to," she says.

"But?"

"I owe it to myself to show up," she says, looking at the glass. "I'm not going to let her deter me from seeing Lighter win the Hopeful."

That is about the last thing I expected to hear, so the squeak of happiness that lifts itself out of my throat surprises us both. When I throw myself at her and wrap her up in my arms, we're doubly surprised.

"Thank you," I tell her. "You won't regret it."

She laughs and pushes me away, poking me in the side with one of her pointy fingers. "Yeah, well, Lighter had better win."

"Count on it," I say, and poke her back.

～

It's late afternoon when I go collect Kali and Maggie out of their paddock. The two have become fast friends in their first day of grazing, standing shoulder to shoulder in the middle of the field, their necks arched to the ground in the single-minded pursuit of eating.

I trek out to the middle of the field. Maggie is the first to look up, because of course she's been expecting me. Kali isn't used to the routine, so she goes on grazing while I fit Maggie with her halter and then rouse Kali's head up from the thick patch of greenery she's been pruning. I snap both lines to their halters and walk back to the gate.

I'm not that shocked to see Dad standing at the fence, one boot propped on the bottom slat and his arms crossed over the top.

"I see you've switched things up with Kali's covert training," he says, giving Kali a once over in that way he looks at all of his horses.

Covert training. So he knew.

"She's mine now," I say, stopping by the fence. Kali's head immediately goes back to the grass, sampling the blades she hasn't gotten around to tasting by the gate. Maggie shoves her head over the fence and into Dad's face, seeking attention and approval and pats on the nose. He gives her all of three before she swings her head back over and butts me in the hip with her forehead.

"I heard that," Dad says, a ghost of a smile on his lips. He's proud, for some reason.

I give him a look.

"Juls, I'm not blind or deaf. I know what you've been up to."

"Could've fooled me," I mutter.

He nods, scuffs the sole of his boot against the fence plank as if trying to dislodge dirt. "I haven't been as forthcoming as I'd like," he admits.

"Try not at all," I say.

"It's been a damn weird summer," he sighs. "I think I owe you an explanation where your mother is concerned."

"She's the best person for the job," I say with a halfhearted shrug. "It's not like I don't get it."

"You shouldn't have to understand it, Juls. You're pissed, and you should be. Putting Mom on Lighter wasn't my sole decision to make," he says. I glance up at him. "I should have talked to you and Martina, and I didn't. I only thought of Lighter, and that wasn't what I should have been doing. I've been far too guilty of putting the horses first, especially since your mother left. I've been disconnected, and that's not how I want things to be anymore."

Something inside me lifts when I hear that, like it's easier to breathe.

"I suppose I didn't realize I was just as bad as your mother in that regard," he says.

"No, you're nothing like her. You're different, and Mom . . . is who she is," I shrug, but that's where I guess I'm wrong because he pins me with an intense stare.

"No, Juls. No way. She's your mother and she lost sight of what was important. She went back on a shitload of promises in search of something she could have easily attained here."

"Then why did she leave?" I ask slowly. "Promises, understandings, your horses to ensure what she wanted . . . why?"

"Your mom," he says, pushing a hand through his thick hair and making it stick up in blond disarray, not unlike Lighter in his finer moments. "Your mom always had her own reasons. She thought there was something in California that she wanted, and she's stubborn enough to stick there."

"Single-minded to a fault," I say. "I think that's what you mean."

"Everything else fades in comparison," he says, and then reaches over the fence to put his hands on both sides of my face. This is familiar, and I remember for a bone-jarring moment that he did the same thing after I caught that brief glimpse of her during the Whirlaway. His fingers catch in my hair, but I don't care. I grip onto the lead ropes of the mares and look him in the eyes, unblinking.

"That may be how she is," he says. "But that doesn't make her justified. She loves you—always will—but she can't bridge the divide she's created, and she knows it. One of these days, she'll figure it out. In the meantime, I don't want to see you defend what she does. Because I see her in you all the time, and you live her kind of life better than she ever has."

My head dips, and I look down, breaking eye contact.

"But that doesn't mean you have to keep doing it, you know," he adds, smoothes his hands over my hair and then lets me go. I stand for a minute, blinking back tears that threaten to spill down my cheeks and watch him open up the gate for me. It takes me a second to gather up the lead ropes and stumble forward, leading the mares out of the paddock. I hand him Kali's lead rope, and he takes the filly while I shut the gate behind us.

I reach up with my free hand and swipe at my eyes, although it doesn't really do any good. "You're right," I say, leading Maggie into the barn and into her stall as Dad does the same with Kali.

"Of course I am," he winks at me over Kali's stall door. "Maybe you can start proving it by going on that vacation Bri keeps hounding you about."

I do a double take. "How did you know about that?"

"Not blind or deaf, remember?" He coils up the lead rope and steps out of Kali's stall. "Besides, Bri isn't exactly quiet about anything."

"This is true." I look down the barn aisle, at its complete state of disarray. "But this is the last year at Blackbridge, and I want to see it to the end."

"See it to the Hopeful," Dad advises, putting an arm around me and squeezing. "We'll end this with a bang."

Chapter Twenty

It's funny. You know how you may want something for days, weeks, months, years and when it's suddenly right there for the taking you don't want it anymore? I feel like that at this very moment. Also, I feel like someone has ripped out my lungs. I'm not sure I can get in a deep enough breath to avoid passing out. The jockeys haven't even arrived in the saddling paddock.

Martina hovers nearby at all times, looking wild and short-tempered. She saves these questioning glances for me every few moments, like she's wordlessly wondering how I am but doesn't have it in her to ask. She may already know, and in fact probably feels the same way I do.

Dad stands off to the side with Delaney and Cynthia. Matthew is making Olivia laugh, pointing at something I don't see. Dad says something I can't hear, and Delaney listens with his head bowed, but Dad is watching us. I wonder if he halfway expects one or both of us to bolt. We probably look like we're ready to run.

I think the magnitude of the situation is lost on Beck, who's standing next to Gus and the colt. Beck is back in his three-piece suit I love so much, probably to the point where I'd like him to never take it off. Gus has managed to cover up all his tattoos with a sports coat I'm sure Izzie forced on him, because he's never comfortable in anything other than cut up shirts and dirty jeans.

Lighter stands with all four feet solidly on the ground, and he looks around like he can't quite focus on any one thing. Beck is distracting the colt, catching his attention with his hand on Lighter's nose, moving when the colt tries to bite his fingers. Gus chuckles and jiggles the lead rope until Lighter lifts a leg and stamps, throwing his head up in frustration at the game.

The paddock thrums with activity, anticipating the last big race of the meet. Ten horses circle around the looping paths that enclose a group of well-dressed onlookers, all except for Lighter, who snorts in irritation. My eyes keep falling on Inventor, a mud-colored colt that hasn't begun to lighten into gray, who moves gentlemanly around the paddock with a swing in his step. The colt's trainer has put another leading rider on him now that Mom backed out, following Lighter like a moth to flame.

I hear Lighter let out a disgruntled snort, followed by a shrill squeal. That's followed by the crack of a hoof against a wooden wall.

Deep down, I have to thank Lighter for dragging my mind to something other than my Mom. I pull my eyes from the chute leading to the jockey's room and move back to Lighter's stall, where my father inspecting the damage Lighter's wreaking on his immediate surroundings. I'm antsy. It's building in my legs and crawling through my skin, like if only I had some room to move I'd be okay. The paddock is almost claustrophobic with the amount of casual race goers crowding the rails.

"Maybe I should walk him around," I he.ar myself announce. Beck gives me a look that outright states I've lost my mind. Gus actually laughs. Dad, however, seems to consider it.

"Gus goes with you," he says, but I expected this. We clip another line onto the colt and lead him out. Lighter goes high stepping forward, fishtailing his hindquarters and eyeing the hoopla surrounding him. I think about that chipmunk, and hope to some higher power that wherever it is, it stays put.

"You okay over there?" Gus asks me while we make the first turn around the loop. Lighter's trying his best to look like he's treading water on land between us, and my arm is already aching from holding him back.

"Dandy." Lighter hauls his head toward Gus, trying to force me around his shoulder. I hold fast and let Gus push the colt into the middle of the pathway.

Gus guides us around the loop and I keep my eyes ahead, my attention on the horse. Lighter floats between us, and it's easy to imagine that it's only our combined weight that tethers him down. It's easy to get lost in the colt while we walk, because Lighter demands every shred of my attention.

It's the stream of colors crossing our path that derails it all.

Lighter lifts his head, and my arms go with him. Gus keeps him going, but my feet are slow to keep up.

Lighter starts to sidestep, pulled in both directions. Finally Gus reaches underneath Lighter's chin and grabs my wrist, shocking me into letting go of the line. The leather snakes onto the ground, and the colt shies. He spins and goes up into the air, a mad streak of copper and blond and flailing hooves.

Gus takes care of it even while I rush to pick up the line. He's already unclipped it from Lighter's equipment, letting it coil down to the ground. The colt dances off, throws his hind legs into the air for good measure, and then continues to move away from me. Gus shoots me an anxious look over his shoulder.

I clench the leather line in my fingers, and walk after Lighter in the wake of the jockeys. Mom is already ensconced within the Blackbridge crowd, her white and black silks peeking through suits and dresses.

Pilar notices me shifting around on the fringe of the group, and slips up next to me.

"How are you holding up?"

I look down at her floral dress and pink high heels, and fiercely wish she was in our silks instead. So that's what I say, and she nods thoughtfully.

"When this cast comes off," she says, "I'm going to make it my personal mission to get back up on that hellion. In the meantime, I'm going to take it as a compliment that the only person they could replace me with is your mother."

Mom is definitely a legend around here. I'll give her that.

Lighter squeals in the background, stamping his hooves like a toddler pitching a fit. Women in spectacular hats turn to consider him, feathers quivering as murmurs rise and fall in the saddling paddock.

"Five weeks," I say, tapping Pilar's cast.

She nods. "Five weeks."

The call for riders up echoes down the line of stalls. The whole paddock becomes a shifting mass of movement and Lighter approaches like a thundering bronze demon, eyes rolling and nostrils flared from the effort of his breaths. Gus keeps him steady, putting a sure hand on his shoulder.

Dad reiterates the plan to Mom, who nods as she tightens the strap on her helmet. Her face is set like stone, a game face I haven't seen in years. It makes something in me turn icy, like I am now being presented with the image I associate with Mom and it's exactly what I expected. She's focused on the horse in front of her, and I remind myself that this is what I asked of her.

Martina stands off to the side, watching impassively as Dad gets Mom's ankle in his hands and boosts her up into the colt's saddle. Lighter shimmies and bobs his head as Mom collects the reins and situates her crop. Then she leans forward over his neck and I want to warn her to stop, but instead of dumping Mom on the ground, Lighter stands like a rock. His ears prick as he studies something in the distance, and Mom threads her fingers through his mane as she whispers to him.

Dios te salve, Maria. Llena eres de gracia: El Señor es contigo.

Then she looks at Martina and me, and something soft breaks through the hard lines on her face. She sits back and smiles.

"It's in the bag," she promises us. I believe her.

She nods once to Gus and they go.

~~

Down below us, a string of two-year-old colts dance next to their outriders. They walk through the mandatory post parade before revving their engines and shifting into pre-flight. Mom lifts herself in the stirrups, cuing Lighter up into a leisurely canter. The colt arches his neck, cocks his head, presses his mouth against the outrider pony's throat.

The box is stifling in the heat and the pressure of waiting for the race.

Beck's got a hand on the middle of my back, and Martina has my hand in a death grip. The rest of our contingent stands in steady anticipation all around me, and I know Gus and Izzie are somewhere down by the rail waiting for the outcome. Saratoga Race Course spreads in front of us, all green and red and brown.

Lighter takes one look at the gate and shies. Mom grabs mane, sitting deeply like she's adhered to the saddle.

"Go in the gate, you little brat," I mutter, mostly to myself. Beck laughs, finding the humor in anything even now.

Lighter puts his head down for one blissful split second and the assistant starters wedge him into his assigned slot. I let out a breath of relief. The horses are in the gate for the Hopeful, and it's only a split second before they charge onto the dirt.

When the bell rings the horses launch out of the gate and rattle around to find room to run. The race is seven furlongs, the length of the backstretch, around the turn, down to the finish. Mom gets Lighter right into the thick of it early, his copper body bounding up along Inventor as they flash along the rail in a headlong sprint for the lead.

I lean forward with the rest of the crowd, watching and waiting and yelling my head off. The horses spill into the turn, Lighter stuck to Inventor's side as they begin to draw away. Mom sits cool and still on his back, feeling for the right time to push the button, but I know that blond monster, and I want him to shake loose and damned well *run*.

Mom lifts her crop and brings it down on his flank, sending Lighter to the front. Inventor drops behind him, dirt from Lighter's shoes flying up into his chest. The rest of the horses bobble and Lighter strides out ahead. Mom puts away the crop and they cruise past the finish line two lengths ahead, Lighter's ears pricked, blond mane flicking askew over his sweaty neck.

I throw my hands up in the air and dance on my toes, bouncing between Martina and Beck as Lighter rounds the first turn with his head down, Mom standing in the stirrups to gently pull him back in.

"What next?" I shout over the crowd as Beck picks me up, turning me around and depositing me on the stairs outside of our box.

"The winner's circle," he says, giving someone a high five over my head and ducking at the slaps on his back.

"That's a tame answer," I accuse, and he shrugs with a smile, leaning down to press his forehead against mine.

"What do you want to hear, July?" he asks, eyes sparking. "Breeders' Cup, Kentucky Derby, Belmont Stakes?"

"Triple Crown," I say, and then press a kiss to his lips. "I expect nothing less."

Dad and Martina cluster behind us, and we hurry down to the track. By the time we get there, Lighter is walking into the circle.

Dad strides up to the colt, putting a hand on his chest. He hesitates before patting Mom on her knee, the two trading silent congratulatory smiles. Lighter takes that moment to crow hop to the side, shaking his head as Gus readjusts his hold on the colt's bridle and straightens him out for the photo.

We cluster as close as we can to the colt, and I drag Martina into it. She hesitantly nestles in by Matthew, throwing him a hesitant smile that he sends back before putting an arm around her shoulders for the camera. Beck grabs my hand and hauls me up to Lighter's head, whispering in my ear, "He wouldn't be here if not for you."

I snort at that, but take the colt's nose in my hand anyway. Lighter rolls one large eye at me and breathes warm over my fingers.

"What do you think?" I ask the colt. "Where to next?

Lighter answers by raking the side of his head along the front of my dress. One swipe down, one swipe up, catching me good on the point of my chin. Gus shoves the colt's head away, and Lighter lifts himself to his full height, turning for the camera.

Beck winces as I tenderly cup my chin, giving him a look.

"I could apologize," he starts, but I only shake my head.

"Don't bother," I say. "I suppose he's worth it."

"See," he grins. "I knew you'd change your tune."

I groan, and face the photographer. We are all lined up, and Lighter is still striking his pose, as if he knows he can't stop until the photograph is taken. Fame is definitely going to go to his head.

Mom smiles brightly, well versed in this part of the game, and leans forward with her left hand resting on the colt's copper shoulder.

And then the camera flashes.

～

It's a joyous occasion to get my feet back in boots, where they belong. The dress goes back in the closet, and I'm back in the barn, also where I belong. The whole place is in the process of being packed up and moved out. Typically we're out of there by dawn, but this time we're dragging our feet.

The sun is setting on Blackbridge. It's all orange and yellow outside, a golden slant to the light that rubs everything in a warm glow. Martina is standing in the doorway of the barn, looking out on it all with her car keys in her hands. My old paddock boots are on the ground by her feet.

"Hey," I say to her as casually as I can.

"I thought I would get a head start," she says, adjusting the strap of her massive bag on her shoulder and turning to face me. "Someone has to go home and wipe up all of the dust before you whirl in there and have a panic attack."

"Not funny," I shake my head.

"I know," she says, leaning down and picking up my boots. "This was definitely not the summer I thought I'd have."

"I can imagine." I take the boots, which are muddy wrecks that I should throw away.

"Do you think you'll go to the Breeders' Cup?"

I frown down at the boots. "I don't know. I guess it depends on if we've got a horse running."

"Lighter is going," Martina laughs, like it's been written in stone and my hesitancy is ridiculous. "Maybe even Galaxy if we've still got her."

"We won't have Galaxy by then," I assure her.

Martina sobers and nods. "Think Mom will ride Lighter again?"

Probably so, but I don't say that. "Not if Pilar has anything to say about it."

Martina's lips lift in a half-smile, although it's not funny at all. Then she pins me with one of her looks. I know them so well. They usually involve a screaming match or a direct order. This time she says, "You should go to the Breeders' Cup this year."

"Why?"

"Because I think we're really past all this, July," she says. "And you want to see Lighter win the Juvy, don't you?"

"If Beck doesn't sell him first," I say. Martina makes a disapproving noise in her throat.

"He'll never sell that horse," she says. "Lighter is taking you to California and Kentucky, Juls."

"I'll believe it when I see it," I say.

Martina flips her keys in her hand. "Oh, you'll see it. Stop being such a downer, Juls."

She opens the door and leans her hip against the inside panel, looking studiously down at the inside of the car for minute. "You think Mom will come back down to Belmont with Dad?"

I consider this, because we've both been giving the apartment a wide berth since the two of them went up there to discuss whatever it is they need to discuss. Martina packed in record time, intent on speeding home to her Mom-free zone. All of that is threatened now with the win in the Hopeful, and I don't know what to tell her. Mom goes where the opportunities are, and Lighter is an opportunity no one would pass up.

"I don't know," I answer honestly. "If she does, it won't be permanent."

"No," Martina nods once, puts on her sunglasses and smiles at me. "It never is."

She pulls me into a hug, my muddy boots stuck between us. "See you at home," she says against my hair, and then releases me.

Martina's car leaves a drifting cloud of dust on the gravel lot, and I walk through it on my way to the barn. I find Dad inside one of the stalls checking out the wraps on one of our two-year-olds. He looks up when I lean against the stall door.

"How did negotiations go?" I ask, nodding up at the loft.

He answers without missing a beat. "Your mother is headed back to California."

"Good," I say, letting out a breath. I try on a smile, and am happy to feel like it fits.

He chuckles then, like what I've said hits home in a way I'll never realize. Or maybe it's that I've finally come to peace with Mom, and he's glad. It has to be something he dealt with ages ago.

"You need me to finish up here?"

"I don't think so, Juls," he says, patting the filly's neck and stepping out of the stall. "In fact, if you stick around here I won't allow you to do a thing. You'll be so bored out of your mind you'll wish you'd gone."

"You're running me off," I say, sounding astonished even to myself.

"No," he corrects me. "I'm making sure you've experienced at least one summer that includes a real vacation. No horses, no tracks, no worrying. Now go get your stuff. If you're lucky you'll be back in the city by the evening. You'll be bound for sun and ocean and all that damn sand in the morning."

"Now?" I ask, eyes wide. "You want me to leave now."

"Did I stutter?" he asks, nudging me between the shoulder blades. "Go on."

I don't have to be told twice.

∿

In the kitchen, Mom is sipping at a glass of red wine and scanning a list of flights on Dad's laptop. She looks over her shoulder as the door thuds closed and pushes away from the counter, looking guilty.

"Find a flight back?" I ask, walking into the loft and beginning to pick up items I've left out.

"Almost," she says, closing the laptop. "I thought I'd help pack things up around here before heading home."

"Good. They'll need an extra hand since I won't be here."

"Where are you going?" Mom comes around the corner, stopping short before she reaches me.

"Back to the city." I pull my suitcase out from the closet and drag it into my bedroom, where Mom follows me.

"Oh," she says, disappointed.

"It's okay." I throw the bag on the bed and begin rooting through dresser drawers, piling clothing into the suitcase haphazardly. "If all goes according to plan, I'll be at the Breeders' Cup at Santa Anita, so you'll see me in two months. Maybe it will be earlier if Lighter races again before Pilar's arm—"

"July," she interrupts. I still, a handful of tank tops in my hands. Mom takes the clothes and puts them in the suitcase, then envelops me in a tight hug.

"You're an amazing girl," she says softly.

I smile against her shoulder, and pat her on the back. She lets me go and takes a big breath.

"Can I help you pack?"

I nod, and pull out the second suitcase from under the bed. "This one is all yours."

It's easy to pull everything together. Mom and I have everything packed up and ready to go in no time flat. Mom brushes away an errant tear after she hugs me again, promising me a room at her house in California over the Breeders' Cup. I know what Martina will say about that, but I promise her that I'll think about it before rolling the last of the suitcases out to my car.

That's where I find Beck.

He's dressed down now, armed folded across his chest, legs crossed at the ankle. His jeans are the old ripped pair, and his T-shirt this time around is so worn it looks like it should be mercifully thrown away. There are frays at every end, but I have a feeling there's no way he'd ever part with it because it proudly proclaims *Fight me, I'm Irish.*

Beck, of course, is grinning like a cat.

Then it dawns on me. "You know about the Outer Banks."

He shrugs, watches me drop the bags in the trunk and slam it closed. "Of course," he says. "We've all known about the Outer Banks. Bri made sure since you'd never go without someone pushing you."

"I take offense at that statement," I say, walking around the car and stopping in front of him. He doesn't look all that concerned, and snags his fingers around my hips, uncrossing his legs and pulling me until I fit between them. I lean against his chest and give him the evil eye.

"I am remarkably okay with that."

That's when I notice his Mustang parked on the other side of my car. "Where are you going?"

"Well," he says, pushing a few loose strands of hair out of my eyes, "when I talked to Bri, she kind of extended the invitation. I think she has this grand idea of double dating and eating seafood by the ocean. It was hard to tell through all the high-pitched gushing."

"When did you start talking to Bri?"

"Oh, early on," he says, to my total astonishment. "I think she's been nursing this beach scenario for at least a few years."

"This is actually an annual thing," I say. "Welcome to Bri's ceaseless meddling."

"Hey," he says, "if someone wants to force excursions on me, I'm all for it. Besides, my horse just won a really big race, so I figure it's deserved."

I laugh. "That's right. You did win a really big race. In fact, you need to get away. Where are you going to go, Beckett Delaney?"

He looks up at the sky, pretending to think about this for a second before swooping down and kissing me. I dig my fingers into his silly, abused shirt and let him in, kissing him there against my car in this sweltering heat. I'm practically flushed with it when he pulls back, lifts a hand to run his thumb over my lips.

"Looks like I'm following you to Queens, July Carter," he says, dropping his hand back down to my hip and pulling me more snuggly against him. A warm rush floods right through me so fast the breath I take catches, and I like the way he looks at me in response. "And after that, I'm apparently car-pooling to North Carolina."

"After that?" I ask. I'm probably being more coy and girly than I usually am.

"Easy," he says, kissing the tip of my nose. "Lighter's going to win the Champagne Stakes."

"Getting overconfident, don't you think?" I ask, pushing him against the side my car.

"In Lighter?" he asks, pushes off the car and spinning us around. The car door is warm against my back, and then there's Beck pressing close. He kisses me quick and says, "Never."

"Would you two stop doing whatever the hell it is you're doing out there and go already?" Izzie yells from the barn. I spot her over Beck's shoulder and groan, hiding my face in his shirt. "You're kind of disgusting all of us, and Gus is too embarrassed to walk outside."

Beck grins and yells over his shoulder, "Gus, dude, stop being such a girl."

I poke Beck hard in the ribs while I hear Gus yell something in Spanish that I can barely make out, most likely defending his honor as a burly man who pushes horses like Lighter around on a daily basis. If the way Izzie erupts into laughter is any indication, she's got some choice thoughts on the subject that she keeps to herself. Beck opens the driver's side door of my car and I take a big breath.

"You ready?"

"Hold on," I say, slipping out from between him and the car. "I'll be back in a second."

I dart back across the parking lot and into the dim barn, striding quickly into Dad's office. The place is a disaster area, papers and folders strewn across the desk and stacked in piles on the floor. Dad is hunting around in one of the filing cabinets, clearly confused. I'm struck, very suddenly, with the need to stay.

"Are you sure?" I ask him, catching him by surprise and watching him drop whatever he's holding back into the cabinet.

"July," he says, "I swear we're fine. Maggie and Kali will be fine. Gus and Izzie and Pilar and everyone else will be fine. I will be fine. Get out of here."

I cross the office and wrap my arms around him, which is a surprise to him. I squeeze him hard.

"Thank you."

"You're welcome," he says, manages to scruff one hand through my hair. I smile and let him go, walking out of the office for the last time.

I stand for a minute in the aisle of the barn, listening to the sounds of the horses. Blackbridge will never be the same after this. It's debatable if I'll ever see Blackbridge again, but I refuse to see this as something tragic. I spot Lighter standing by his stall door, his bright copper head glinting in the evening sun that spills into the barn. His shock of white-blond mane sits in unruly chaos along the line of his neck, and he watches me expectantly, waiting for something.

This colt is going to win the Champagne Stakes. He'll go on to California and Kentucky, and we'll be with him, watching. We'll witness him recreate our lives with every step he takes on the track, and in some ways he'll be the colt that started it all. I know I'll be there to see it, no matter where he goes.

I look out at the farm behind the doors of the barn. The gravel road sits quietly in the summer haze, waiting for me to drive over it and never come back. It's exhilarating, being presented with a different course, options, a fragile beginning to a different life in which I'm not afraid of deviation.

Maybe, if things go right, I'll go to California.

Lighter whinnies loudly at nothing, accenting his scream with a crack of hooves against solid wood. I come back to myself, to Lighter twisting his neck and tossing his wild mane in all directions. His eyes are bright, full of promises.

I take a big, big breath.

Then I walk out of the barn and back into the dying Saratoga light.

About the Author

Mara Dabrishus is an author and librarian who lives in Cleveland, Ohio. Horse racing is her first great love, but for the past several years she's ridden dressage, learning how to spiral in, half halt, and perform the perfect figure eight. She is also the author of *Finding Daylight* and two short stories: *Whirlaway* and *Saratoga Summers*.

She can be found blogging about horses, racing, writing and everything in between at www.maradabrishus.com.

Acknowledgments

I wouldn't have been able to get *Stay the Distance* off the ground without Maggie Dana, who encouraged me to publish. Erin Smith, my editor and copy editor, read and re-read the manuscript and never once complained. A huge shout-out goes to my group of beta readers, especially the two who have been with me forever: Carrie Starkey and Monique Bernic. Thank you to Sandra and Rick Fritzinger, who invited me to tag along with them to Saratoga for one glorious week so I could see the hoopla around the Travers Stakes and take a trillion photos. Then there is my family, who without fail has always encouraged this madness.

CPSIA information can be obtained
at www.ICGtesting.com
Printed in the USA
LVOW04s1946151116

513060LV00010B/1252/P